Shine

Judy Garton-Sprenger • Philip Prowse
Dioni Davids • Hara Yiannakopoulou

Grammar
Book 3

MACMILLAN

MAP OF THE BOOK

Irregular Verbs

Infinitive	Past simple	Past participle
be	was, were	been
beat	beat	beaten
become	became	become
begin	began	begun
bend	bent	bent
bet	bet	bet
bite	bit	bitten
bleed	bled	bled
blow	blew	blown
break	broke	broken
bring	brought	brought
broadcast	broadcast	broadcast
build	built	built
burn	burnt/burned	burnt/burned
buy	bought	bought
catch	caught	caught
choose	chose	chosen
come	came	come
cost	cost	cost
cut	cut	cut
do	did	done
draw	drew	drawn
dream	dreamt/dreamed	dreamt/dreamed
drink	drank	drunk

Infinitive	Past simple	Past participle
drive	drove	driven
eat	ate	eaten
fall	fell	fallen
feed	fed	fed
feel	felt	felt
fight	fought	fought
find	found	found
fly	flew	flown
forget	forgot	forgotten
freeze	froze	frozen
get	got	got
give	gave	given
grow	grew	grown
go	went	gone
hang	hung	hung
have	had	had
hear	heard	heard
hide	hid	hidden
hit	hit	hit
hold	held	held
hurt	hurt	hurt
keep	kept	kept
know	knew	known
lay	laid	laid

Irregular Verbs

Infinitive	Past simple	Past participle
lead	led	led
learn	learnt/learned	learnt/learned
leave	left	left
lend	lent	lent
let	let	let
lie	lay	lain
light	lit	lit
lose	lost	lost
make	made	made
mean	meant	meant
meet	met	met
pay	paid	paid
put	put	put
read	read	read
ride	rode	ridden
ring	rang	rung
rise	rose	risen
run	ran	run
say	said	said
see	saw	seen
sell	sold	sold
send	sent	sent
set	set	set
shake	shook	shaken

Infinitive	Past simple	Past participle
shine	shone	shone
shoot	shot	shot
show	showed	shown
smell	smelt/smelled	smelt/smelled
shut	shut	shut
speak	spoke	spoken
speed	sped	sped
spell	spelt/spelled	spelt/spelled
spend	spent	spent
spoil	spoilt/spoiled	spoilt/spoiled
stand	stood	stood
steal	stole	stolen
stick	stuck	stuck
swim	swam	swum
take	took	taken
teach	taught	taught
tear	tore	torn
tell	told	told
think	thought	thought
throw	threw	thrown
understand	understood	understood
wake	woke	woken
wear	wore	worn
win	won	won
write	wrote	written

LESSON 1 · *It's a fabulous day, isn't it?*

1 Question tags

We use **question tags** with falling intonation to ask the listener to agree that something is true.

> He's happy, **isn't he?**
> She can ride a bike, **can't she?**
> They didn't arrive yesterday, **did they?**

We make **question tags** with the auxilary verb and pronoun.

Remember -
If the main part of the sentence is **affirmative**, we use a **negative** question tag.

> They must do their homework, **mustn't they?**

If the main part of the sentence is **negative**, we use an **affirmative** question tag.

> They haven't got a dog, **have they?**

Top Tip!

To form question tags in the **present simple** or the **past simple** tenses we use the auxilary verb that these tenses use when they are in the negative or question form – as **do** and **does** (present simple), **did** (past simple).

> She always asks a lot of questions, **doesn't she?**
> She went to the theatre yesterday, **didn't she?**

2 Gerunds

We form the **gerund** by adding **–ing** to the end of the verb.
The **gerund** is used after these verbs: *like, love, enjoy, hate, can't stand.*

> She loves **skiing.**
> I can't stand **drinking** milk in the morning.

We use the **gerund** after the verb **go** when we are talking about sport.

> We go **swimming** every Sunday.

We can also use **gerunds** after prepositions:

> I feel like **having** a rest.
> Carl is keen on **going** to the cinema.
> I look forward to **seeing** you soon.

1 Complete the sentences with question tags.

0   They are getting married soon, *aren't they?*

1   Cats don't like getting wet, _____?

2   Your sister didn't give you a birthday present, _____?

3   He likes doing watersports, _____?

4   You didn't phone, _____?

5   Jim wasn't really ill, _____?

6   Dolphins can stay underwater longer than us, _____?

2 Complete the sentences with gerunds. Use these verbs.

go   have   listen   study   ~~tell~~   visit   watch

0 He loves *telling* jokes to make people laugh.
1 He hates _____ geography at school.
2 Dogs can't stand _____ baths.
3 I feel like _____ to the beach.
4 She enjoys _____ her grandparents in the country.
5 Tom is looking forward to _____ a film tonight on TV.
6 He enjoys _____ to music.

3 Complete the second sentence so that it means the same as the first one.

0 Jenny is very interested in collecting stamps. (keen)
   Jenny is *keen on* collecting stamps.
1 The dog is ill. It doesn't want to eat anything. (feel)
   The dog is ill. It doesn't _____ anything.
2 He hates taking the bus into town. (can't)
   He _____ the bus into town.

3 The children are excited about the party tomorrow. (look)
   The children _____ the party tomorrow.
4 Mike wants to go mountain climbing. (interested)
   Mike _____ mountain climbing.
5 I swim every day during the holidays. (go)
   I _____ every day during the holidays.

4 Complete the text with the correct answers.

Harrison Ford is one of today's most famous actors. When he feels like (0) *escaping* from New York, he flies with his family to his country house in Wyoming. He really loves (1) _____ his private plane. All the family look forward (2) _____ spending their holidays there. They enjoy (3) _____ in a nearby river. They also (4) _____ walking in the mountains.

Harrison Ford came from a poor family. He was always keen (5) _____ becoming an actor and left college without (6) _____ his studies. He went to Hollywood where he worked as a carpenter. He tried to get parts in films but hated (7) _____ polite to the directors. Then his friend George Lucas gave him a role in the film *Star Wars*, which made him famous. He also loved (8) _____ Indiana Jones.

Ford is interested (9) _____ keeping fit and healthy. He also (10) _____ living a quiet, private life away from the bright lights of Hollywood.

0	a. <u>escaping</u>	b. is escaping	c. escapes
1	a. flies	b. flying	c. is flying
2	a. at	b. in	c. to
3	a. fish	b. to fish	c. fishing
4	a. going	b. go	c. are going
5	a. on	b. in	c. at

6	a. finish	b. finishing	c. finishes
7	a. to be	b. to being	c. being
8	a. plays	b. playing	c. played
9	a. to	b. in	c. on
10	a. liking	b. being	c. likes

LESSON 2 *I didn't mean to laugh*

Verb + infinitve

We use the infinitive after certain verbs:

> agree ask decide know how manage mean need pretend
> promise refuse offer seem try want would like

Mark agreed **to try**.
Alison decided **to go** to bed.
Rick knows **how to** windsurf.
Mark is **learning to** swim.
Holly **managed to** save Mark.
What do you mean **to say**?
I need **to wash** my hands.
Lucy refused **to listen**.

Tara offered **to teach** Mark.
Mark didn't pretend **to be** in trouble.
She promised **to help** him.
They seem **to be** happy.
We are trying **to finish** the puzzle.
Do you want **to start**?
I'd like **to watch** the video.

With some verbs, for example, ask, teach, want and tell, we can put the object/person before the infinitive so that we know who is going to do the action in the **infinitive**.

   Alison asked Tara **to give** her a glass of water.
(Tara is going to give Alison the water.)
   She told me **to make** some coffee.
(I am going to make her some coffee.)
   I want you **to close** the window.
(you are going to close the window.)
   Tara is teaching Mark **to swim**.
(Mark is learning to swim).

---

1 Tick the correct sentences.

0   *The thief agreed to give back the stolen money.* ✔

1   Bill wanted to look good for the party. ☐

2   Nick pretends to being ill when

    he doesn't want to study. ☐

3   Our teacher can talk about himself for hours. ☐

4   People go ski in the mountains in winter. ☐

5   We are going to visit the zoo tomorrow. ☐

6   Aliki is looking forward to doing watersports. ☐

7   The baby can't to walk yet; it's too young. ☐

8   The workers refused do any extra work. ☐

2 Complete the sentences with infinitives. Use these verbs.

> do find help know look ~~panic~~

HOW TO BE A SUCCESSFUL STUDENT

0   Try not *to panic* during exams.

1   Don't pretend _____ the answer when you

    don't.

2   Offer _____ younger students when you can.

3   Try _____ your homework on time.

4   Don't forget _____ at your notes regularly.

5   Remember _____ free time to do some

    fun things.

3 Complete the second sentence so that it means the same as the first one.

0 She should study harder to pass the exams. (need)

She *needs* to study harder to pass the exams.

1 The shop assistant gave me the wrong money by accident. (mean)

The shop assistant didn't _____ me the wrong money.

2 I don't really want to go out in the cold. (feel)

I don't really _____ out in the cold.

3 Now try to capsize the canoes. (practise)

Now _____ the canoes.

4 My best friend knows how to play the piano well. (can)

My best friend _____ piano well.

5 'Can I help you with your homework?' (offered)

Sally _____ the student with her homework.

4 Complete the text with the correct answers.

The Theatre

Nobody seems (0) *to know* exactly when people started (1) _____ write plays and to act.

However, we do know that the Ancient Greeks were the first (2) _____ theatres.

They knew how to build them so that everybody in the audience could (3) _____

and (4) _____ the actors. All the actors were men and some had to pretend

(5) _____ women for some roles.

People loved (6) _____ to the theatre and even poor people (7) _____

go because there were free seats for them. One of the most famous Athenian dramatists was Sophocles

(496-406 BC) who managed (8) _____ 123 plays. There were many kinds of plays

(9) _____ tragedies, historical dramas and comedies. Many of these plays are still performed

today. People are still very keen (10) _____ going to the theatre even though we now have

television and the cinema.

0	a. knows	b. to know	c. knowing	6	a. go	b. going	c. to going
1	a. to	b. too	c. two	7	a. can't	b. can	c. could
2	a. building	b. to building	c. to build	8	a. writing	b. to write	c. write
3	a. to see	b. to seeing	c. see	9	a. see	b. seeing	c. to see
4	a. hear	b. to hear	c. hearing	10	a. in	b. on	c. about
5	a. be	b. being	c. to be				

5 Complete these sentences about yourself.

1 I would like to _____

2 I refuse to _____

3 I promised to _____

4 I try to _____

5 I sometimes pretend to _____

6 In the future I will know how to _____

LESSON 3   *Try harder!*

---

❶ Comparison of adverbs

Adverbs of manner tell us *how* something happens.
We usually form **adverbs of manner** by adding **–ly** to the end of adjectives.
quick ➔ quick**ly**

But there are some rules you need to remember:

- For adjectives that end in **y** – take away the **–y** and add **–ily** to make the adverb.
  happy ➔ happ**ily**

- For some adjectives that end in **–e** – take away the **e** and then add **–ly** (or just **–y** if the word already has **l** at the end) to make the adverb.
  miserable ➔ miserab**ly**

- Remember to learn the irregular adverbs.
  good ➔ **well**
  hard ➔ **hard**
  fast ➔ **fast**
  early ➔ **early**
  late ➔ **late**

Like adjectives, **adverbs** also have **comparative** and **superlative** forms.
For **comparative adverbs** we usually use **more** + adverb.
  Amy works **more quickly** than Sarah.

For **superlative adverbs** we usually use **the most** + adverb.
  Karen works **the most quickly** of all the students.

Look at how we make the **comparative** and **superlative** of some **irregular adverbs**.
well ➔ **better** ➔ **(the) best**
badly ➔ **worse** ➔ **(the) worst**
hard ➔ **harder** ➔ **(the) hardest**
fast ➔ **faster** ➔ **(the) fastest**
  Tara swims **faster** than Rick.
  Alison swims the **fastest** of all the teachers.

> **Top Tip!**
> Remember to use the word **than** after the comparative.

❷ Adverbs of degree

These adverbs are followed by an adjective or another adverb
– **quite**, **very**, **really**, **extremely**, **incredibly**.
  She is **extremely** beautiful.
  That train goes **incredibly** fast.

---

❶   Tick the correct box.

		Adjective	Adverb
0	That car goes *faster* than yours.	☐	✓
00	The students are extremely *noisy* this afternoon.	✓	☐
1	He speaks French very *well*. His mother is from France.	☐	☐
2	The mother held her baby *gently*.	☐	☐
3	The student tried *harder* this year at school.	☐	☐
4	John is *the fastest* swimmer in the school.	☐	☐
5	This is *the most incredible* thing I've ever seen.	☐	☐

2 Complete the chart.

	Adjective	Comparative adjective	Superlative adjective	Adverb	Comparative adverb	Superlative adverb
0	slow	*slower*	*the slowest*	*slowly*	*more slowly*	*the most slowly*
00	fast	*faster*	*the fastest*	*fast*	*faster*	*the fastest*
1	quiet	_____	_____	_____	_____	_____
2	noisy	_____	_____	_____	_____	_____
3	happy	_____	_____	_____	_____	_____
4	miserable	_____	_____	_____	_____	_____
5	bad	_____	_____	_____	_____	_____
6	good	_____	_____	_____	_____	_____
7	safe	_____	_____	_____	_____	_____
8	dangerous	_____	_____	_____	_____	_____
9	warm	_____	_____	_____	_____	_____
10	cold	_____	_____	_____	_____	_____

3 Complete the sentences with adverbs from the chart above.

0 He did very *well* in the history test.

1 You can travel _____ by plane than by car.

2 Talk _____ or you'll wake up the baby.

3 Make sure you dress _____ today because it's snowing.

4 The little girl smiled _____ when she saw the ice cream.

5 At the concert, we all shouted _____ .

6 The lost puppy was crying _____ .

4 Write sentences.

0 Ricky Martin/good/than better my dad.
Ricky Martin dances better than my dad.

1 Gabrielle/sing/extremely/good

_____

2 Mike/run/very/quick

_____

3 Tom/speak/French/good/than his sister

_____

4 Sarah/do/her homework/careful/than other children

_____

5 I/get up/late/than my mother

_____

LESSON 4 *Use Your Grammar*

We use **so** and **but** as linking words to connect two ideas. We use **but** to contrast two ideas:
    I'm from Argentina.
    At the moment I'm on holiday in England.
    I'm from Argentina **but** at the moment I'm on holiday in England.

We use **so** to talk about consequence or result.
    I've lived in the same town all my life.
    I know lots of people there.
    I've lived in the same town all my life **so** I know lots of people there.

Look at these examples:
    I like boys **but** I don't like talking about football.
    Email is easier than letters **so** please give me your email address.

1   **Vicky wrote an article about her teacher for the school magazine.**
    First she interviewed the teacher and made notes.
    Then she wrote the article.

Look at the notes Vicky made
when she interviewed her teacher.

Name	: Miss Pitts
From	: Australia
Loves	: walking dog/beach
Really likes	: local restaurants (because not good at cooking)
Enjoys	: cinema
Not keen on	: theatre – why?
Can't stand	: swimming in cold sea/smoking – feels sick
Looks forward to	: birthday and holidays
Sometimes feels like	: escaping from the city
Offers students	: help with problems
Tells students	: truth
Is unhappy	: when students behave badly or are late

4

2 Now read the article.

Our English Teacher

Our English teacher is called Miss Pitts and she's from Australia.
I asked her about her life and what she likes doing when she's not
working. Sometimes she feels like escaping from the city so she goes
to a nearby beach where she loves walking her dog. She likes the sea,
but can't stand swimming when the water is cold. The other thing she
really hates is smoking – the smell makes her feel sick.

In the evening she enjoys going to the cinema, but she's not keen on
the theatre. She didn't tell me why. She really likes having dinner in
local restaurants because she's not very good at cooking, and she
looks forward to her birthday and the holidays.

At school she tells her students the truth and and always offers to
help students with problems. She's unhappy when the students
behave badly or are late. She enjoys teaching and I hope she'll stay at
our school for a long time.

3 Interview someone you know about what they like and don't like
doing, and make notes.

Then write an article about them using your notes.

_____

_____

_____

_____

LESSON 5 | *Test Yourself*

1 Complete the sentences with question tags. Guess the animal.

0 It lives in the sea, *doesn't it?*

1 It isn't a fish, _____ ?

2 It has got a long nose, _____ ?

3 These animals are fast swimmers, _____ ?

4 They live in groups, not alone, _____ ?

5 They like human beings, _____ ?

6 But they don't like sharks, _____ ?

7 It can communicate using special sounds, _____ ?

8 It's a _____ , isn't it?

2 Complete the sentences with the correct form of the word in brackets.

0 The dog always barks *angrily* at the postman. (angry)

1 Alice did extremely _____ in the test. (good)

2 The cat is eating _____ . (hungry)

3 It is _____ to travel by plane than by car. (quick)

4 Which animal can run _____ ? (fast)

5 Look! That bird is flying _____ than the plane. (high)

6 Students who are interested in their lessons learn _____ than students who aren't. (easy)

7 He is _____ swimmer in the class. (bad)

3 Complete the sentences with gerunds or infinitives.

0 Some people are keen on *doing* dangerous sports like parachuting. (do)

1 The teacher agreed _____ us less homework for the weekend. (give)

2 My sister is very bossy! She enjoys _____ me what to do. (tell)

3 Do you look forward to _____ new friends at summer camp? (make)

4 I didn't mean _____ , but you look so funny in those clothes. (laugh)

5 He wants everything to be perfect. He hates _____ mistakes. (make)

6 The climbers managed _____ the top of the mountain. (reach)

7 Mike goes _____ when the weather is good. (swim)

8 Do you promise _____ in touch when you move house? (keep)

9 Would you like _____ me a hand with the housework? (give)

10 I love _____ letters in my free time. (write)

4 Underline the correct answer.

0 The divers didn't find the treasure, **didn't they?/they did/<u>did they?</u>**

1 Martin decided **to phone/phoning/not phone** us because he was going to be late.

2 Young people hope **to change/to changing/changing** the world when they grow up.

3 Their train arrived **early/earlier/earliest** than we thought.

4 My dog is very lazy. He never feels like **play/playing/to play**.

5 He can't stand **being/to being/be** alone. He wants people around him.

6 You need **taking/taking/to take** a deep breath before diving.

7 Thompson won the gold medal for the 200 metre race because he ran **the most fastest/ the fastest/the faster**.

5 Complete the text with the correct answers.

SEA WORLD

Sea World is a famous sea park in Florida, USA. It has a wide variety of animals like sharks, dolphins, seals, penguins and even killer whales! There are many fascinating things (0) *to see* and do.

Watching these animals perform in shows is (1) _____ amazing! They also enjoy (2) _____ audiences what they can do. Shamu, a killer whale, is the star of the show. She loves (3) _____ the water with her tail and splashing people at the front. So if you don't feel like (4) _____ wet, sit further away. When the dolphins perform they try (5) _____ as high as they can before diving into the pool again.

Special trainers teach these animals how (6) _____ these tricks, which is (7) _____ difficult. These people also look after them and have a very special friendship with them. You can ask (8) _____ the dolphins, if you're not afraid, of course. But for visitors who want to live more (9) _____, there are sharks in a special pool. You can come face to face with them. But don't worry, there is a glass wall between you and them. So you don't need (10) _____ scared!

0	a. see	b. to see	c. seeing	d. to seeing
1	a. real	b. more really	c. really	d. most really
2	a. showing	b. to showing	c. to show	d. show
3	a. hit	b. hitting	c. to hitting	d. hits
4	a. getting	b. to get	c. get	d. to getting
5	a. jump	b. to jump	c. to jumping	d. jumps
6	a. doing	b. do	c. to doing	d. to do
7	a. extreme	b. extremely	c. most extremely	d. more extremely
8	a. feeding	b. to feed	c. feed	d. to feeding
9	a. dangerous	b. danger	c. dangerously	d. most danger
10	a. be	b. being	c. to being	d. to be

LESSON 1 *She won't talk to you*

Future review: *will* and *going to*

We can use **will** and **going to** to talk about the future.
How do we decide which one to use? It depends on what we are talking about.

❶ *Will*

● Things we hope or predict will happen.
When I grow up I'**ll be** rich and famous.

● Promises.
Don't worry. I **will give** you your bike back soon.

● Decisions made at the time of speaking.
I think I'**ll have** a coffee.

❷ *Going to*

● Plans or intentions for the future.
I'**m going to** visit my grandparents this weekend.

● Things we believe will happen because we have proof or evidence at the time of speaking.
The sky is dark. It'**s going to** rain.

❶ Match.

A

0	The baby is afraid to walk	d
1	The sun will	
2	The teacher won't	
3	She is going	
4	Is he going	
5	It's summer and there will	
6	The football team is going to	

B

a.   help the students during the test.

b.   to meet her penfriend next week.

c.   come up at 6 am tomorrow.

d.   ~~because it thinks it will fall over.~~

e.   be a lot of people on the beach.

g.   train very hard for the championship.

f.   to invite Alison to his party?

❷ Complete the sentences with *will/won't* or *going to/not going to*.

0   It's so cold! I think it *is going to* snow.

1   I _____ pay you back the money tomorrow, I promise!

2   The fortune teller said: 'You _____ become famous.'

3   I _____ be late back home, don't worry.

4   I'm really hot and thirsty. I think I _____ have a cold drink.

5   I don't feel very well. I _____ to be sick!

3 **Complete the text with the correct form of these verbs.**

| be do fall in love live meet ~~not be~~ not want see study travel write |

Yesterday I met a fortune teller at the fair. This is what she told me.

Fortune teller: You (0) *won't be* rich and famous but you (1) _____ happy. Happy and poor.

Me: But I (2) _____ to be poor. How do you know all these things?

Fortune teller: I can (3) _____ it all here in your hand! You (4) _____ medicine to become a doctor.

Me: A doctor? Me? But I've already decided what I (5) _____ .
I (6) _____ around the world and become a famous explorer,
and I (7) _____ lots of travel books.

Fortune teller: I can promise you two things. Firstly, you (8) _____ a wonderful person and the two of you (9) _____ and secondly, (10) _____ happily ever after.

Me: Oh, that's all very nice, but can you look again to see if there's a little money somewhere?

4 **Write**

A. Four promises to your best friend.

1 _____
2 _____
3 _____
4 _____

B. Four hopes for your future.

1 _____
2 _____
3 _____
4 _____

C. Four things you've already arranged to do.

1 _____
2 _____
3 _____
4 _____

D. Four things you can see are going to happen.

1 _____
2 _____
3 _____
4 _____

LESSON 2   *What have you two been doing?*

1 Present perfect continuous

We form the **present perfect continuous** with the verb **be** in the **present perfect** tense + the main verb with the ending **–ing**.

Affirmative	**Negative**	**Questions**
I have been running	I haven't been running	Have I been running?
you have been running	you haven't been running	Have you been running?
he has been running	he hasn't been running	Has he been running?
she has been running	she hasn't been running	Has she been running?
it has been running	it hasn't been running	Has it been running?
we haven't been running	we haven't been running	Have we been running?
you have been running	you haven't been running	Have you been running?
they have been running	they haven't been running	Have they been running?

Short answers

Yes, I have./No, I haven't.   Yes, it has./No, it hasn't.
Yes, you have./No, you haven't.   Yes, we have./No, we haven't.
Yes, he has./No, he hasn't.   Yes, you have./No, you haven't.
Yes, she has./No, she hasn't.   Yes, they have./No, they haven't.

Top Tip!

Use **has** for the third person singular (he/she/it).
Change the word order for questions.

We can use the **present perfect continuous** to describe actions that started in the past and have continued until now:
> He**'s been studying** hard.
> (He started at 9 o'clock this morning and it is now 2 o'clock and he is still studying.)

We can also use the present perfect continuous to describe actions that started in the past and finished a short time ago, but with a result we can see in the present:
> He**'s been eating chocolate**.
> (He isn't eating chocolate now but there is chocolate round his mouth!)

2 *for/since*

We often use **for** and **since** with the **present perfect continuous**.

We use **for** when we are talking about **how long**.
> I**'ve been watching** TV **for** an hour.

We use **since** when we are talking about **when** something started.
> I**'ve been watching** TV **since** six o'clock.

3 Present perfect simple and present perfect continuous

We usually use the **present perfect simple** to talk about actions and events that took place at an indefinite time in the past.
> I **have done** my homework.
> (I did it at some time before now.)

We usually use the **present perfect continuous** to talk about actions that started in the past and have not finished yet.
> I **have been doing** my homework for hours.
> (I am still doing it.)

1 Complete the sentences using the present perfect simple.

0 I'm so hungry! I *haven't eaten* anything all day. (not eat)

1 Tom is late. I'm sure he _____ the bus again. (miss)

2 Betty _____ to become a doctor since she was a little girl. (want)

3 They _____ everything for their holiday. They're ready to go. (plan)

4 How many tourists _____ the Pyramids this year? (visit)

5 He _____ his new car for a week. (have)

2 Complete the sentences with *for* or *since*.

0 John has been learning Spanish *for* a few years.

1 I have known my best friend _____ I was six years old.

2 He has been working on that old car _____ about six months.

3 Have they been living here _____ 1990?

4 Mrs Brown has been teaching at our school _____ three years.

5 Where have you been? I've been waiting here _____ two o'clock!

3 Complete the sentences with the present perfect continuous.

0 The same postman *has been delivering* our letters for the last ten years. (deliver)

1 I _____ my room for hours, but I haven't finished yet. (tidy up)

2 His dog _____ since last week and he's very worried. (miss)

3 I haven't watched any television because I _____ my homework since I got home. (do)

4 She is a famous writer. She _____ books since 1958. (write)

5 How long _____ your birthday party? For a month! (you/plan)

4 Complete the sentences with the present perfect simple or continuous.

0 We *haven't seen* Alison since the party last Saturday. (not see)

1 That young boy keeps having accidents. He _____ three so far. (have)

2 When is the doctor coming? I _____ for forty minutes. (wait)

3 The price of food _____ ever since the beginning of the year. (increase)

4 The main news on the TV _____ . Now it's time for the local news. (finish)

5 I think you _____ your leg. Let me take you to hospital. (break)

6 George has a headache because he _____ since this morning. (study)

7 That girl lives in the mountains and she _____ the sea. (never see)

8 We _____ housework all day and we haven't finished yet. (do)

9 Germany and Italy _____ the World Cup three times since 1930. (win)

10 Millions of people _____ to school and can't read or write. (never be)

LESSON 3 *Believe in yourself*

1 Reflexive pronouns

We use **reflexive pronouns** when the subject and the object of the verb in the sentence are the same.

The **reflexive pronouns** are –
myself
yourself
himself
herself
itself
ourselves
yourselves
themselves

We put **reflexive pronouns** after the verb.
He enjoyed **himself** last night.

We often use reflexive pronouns after these verbs: **believe in, behave, enjoy, help, hurt, look after**.
Do you believe in **yourself**?
He didn't behave **himself** last night.
We enjoyed **ourselves** at the party.
Will you help **yourself** to some coffee?
She hurt **herself** really badly.
Don't worry about them. They always look after **themselves**.

2 How often and adverbial phrases of frequency

When we want to say **how often** something happens, we can use **adverbial phrases of frequency**.
How often do you go to the cinema?
I go to the cinema **once a week**.

How often does Laura play tennis?
She plays tennis **twice a month**.

How often do you go to London?
I go ten **times a** year.

How often does Ben play football?
He plays **every Sunday**.

How often do you see your grandparents?
I see them **most weekends**.

How often does Millie go swimming?
She goes swimming **every morning** and **some evenings**.

1 Complete the sentences with a reflexive pronoun.

0   She couldn't wait for dinner so she helped *herself* to some food.

1   At the hairdresser's you can't help looking at _____ in the mirror.

2   He failed his geography exam and was ashamed of _____.

3   Sometimes when people are lonely they talk to _____.

4   My friend and I can speak French. We taught _____.

5   The child is very young and can't look after _____.

6   You and Rick have many talents. You should believe in _____.

7   I hope I will enjoy _____ at the rock concert.

8   She always enjoys _____ on holiday.

2 Complete the second sentence so that it means the same as the first one. Use the words in brackets and a reflexive pronoun.

0   He doesn't care about other people. (thinks of)
He only thinks of himself.

1   The driver knew the accident was his fault. (blamed)
The driver _____ for the accident.

2 We had a great time during the summer holidays. (enjoyed)

We _____ during the summer holidays.

3 The children were very good at the party. (behaved)

The children _____ at the party.

4 They did all the work. (by)

They did all the work _____. Nobody helped them.

5 Mary passed all her exams and was really pleased. (proud of)

Mary was _____ for passing all her exams.

3 Answer these questions.

1 How often do you go to the cinema? _____

2 How often does your brother/sister shout at you? _____

3 How often do you listen to your favourite music? _____

4 How often do you have English lessons? _____

5 How often do you see your friends? _____

4 Write questions using *How often*. Then ask a friend and write the answers.

How often…   you/do/your homework   you/eat/pizza

you/read/books   you/visit/your grandparents

you/go/to the cinema   you/buy/clothes

Question   **Answer**

0 *How often do you do your homework?*   *Nick never does his homework.*

1 _____   _____

2 _____   _____

3 _____   _____

4 _____   _____

5 _____   _____

5 Look at the answers and write questions.

0 How often *did you go to the cinema last month?*   I went to the cinema twice last month.

1 How often _____?   The two brothers fight almost every day.

2 How often _____?   I never eat Chinese food.

3 How often _____?   The athlete is going to train once a day.

4 How often _____?   They will write to each other every week.

5 How often _____?   My sister phones her friend three times a day.

LESSON 4 *Use Your Grammar*

Before you write a personal description, it's best to plan what you're going to say.
You can describe the different times of the person's life – what they did when they were younger, what their situation is now, what they usually/always do, and what they will do in the future.

You use different **tenses** to describe the different times of their life
- **present simple** to write about what they usually/always do
- **present perfect** to write about things they have done at an indefinite time in the past
- **past simple** to write about what they did at a specific time in the past
- **will** and **going to** to write about their plans and hopes for the future

1 **Complete the passage by writing the verbs in brackets in the correct tense.**

My Best Friend.

My best friend, Daisy, (1) _____ (be) a great person. I (2) _____ (know) her for a very long time because our mothers (3) _____ (be) friends when they were young. I remember Daisy as a little girl. She (4) _____ (play) with me three or four times a week when we were both three years old. She (5) _____ (share) her toys with me and we (6) _____ (have) a lot of fun together then.

Daisy is an extremely pretty girl. She always (7) _____ (look) nice and she (8) _____ (wear) lovely clothes. She (9) _____ (work) hard at school and sometimes she (10) _____ (help) me with my homework. She (11) _____ (love) travelling and she (12) _____ (go) to at least seven different countries so far. She (13) _____ (go) to America next month and she hopes she (14) _____ (work) as a teacher when she grows up. I'd love you to meet Daisy. She's brilliant!

2 **Read this text about Vicky's grandmother.**
Write down the tense of each numbered verb.

I'd like to tell you about my grandmother because I think she (1) **is** a very special person. She was born a really long time ago in a village in the mountains. When she (2) **was** ten years old her mother (3) **died** and she had to look after her little brothers and sisters. The family was very poor and she couldn't go to school any more, but she (4) **taught** herself many things from the books the teacher (5) **gave** her. Soon my grandmother (6) **became** a young woman.

One day, she (7) **saw** a tall, good-looking stranger walking around the village. He stopped to ask her a question and they talked for a long time. He told her that he wanted to see the village because his best friend's family was from there. (8) 'I**'ve** always **wanted** to see the village,' the man said. (9) He **liked** talking to her because she was clever and knew a lot of things about the village. (She was also very beautiful!). They (10) **met** every day and after a couple of months he asked her to marry him. (11) '**I'm going to make** you very happy,' he told her, 'and I promise I (12) **will look after** your family.'

They (13) **have been** together ever since that day and (14) **are** very happy, but life (15) **has not always been** easy for them. Grandfather was badly hurt in the war, but he kept his promises to my grandmother. He sent her brothers and sisters to university and she went back to school to become a teacher. Then she opened a library so that everyone could read books and learn, even if they came from poor families.

1   *present simple*

2   _____

3   _____

4   _____

5   _____

6   _____

7   _____

8   _____

9   _____

10 _____

11 _____

12 _____

13 _____

14 _____

15 _____

3 **Now write about someone you think is special.**
    Think carefully about which tenses you use and why.

_____

_____

_____

_____

_____

_____

_____

_____

LESSON 5 — Test Yourself

1 Complete the sentences with the 'will' future of these verbs.

| beat bite have help hit promise |

0   I bet he *will beat* me at chess. He's really good.

1   _____ you _____ to be good children until I come back?

2   Don't touch that dog. He _____ you!

3   The weather forecast says a terrible storm _____ this area tomorrow.

4   _____ you _____ me do this exercise, please? I can't do it on my own.

5   I've changed my mind. I _____ that ice cream!

2 Complete the sentences with a reflexive pronoun.

0   My dad says that if you want to be happy, you have to believe in *yourself.*

1   His mother said, 'if you want to do it by _____ , without my help, then go ahead.'

2   The workers injured _____ when they cut down the trees.

3   Helen blamed _____ for her problems and nobody else.

4   Nobody could believe I painted the room by _____ .

5   The new student wanted to introduce _____ , but she was too shy.

6   The washing machine turns _____ off.

7   We were really enjoying _____ in the park, when it started to rain.

3 Complete the dialogue with ONE word in each space.

Tina: Hello Sarah! You look happy.

Sarah: I am. I have (0) *had* an extremely interesting weekend.

Tina: Are you (1) _____ to tell me about it?

Sarah: Of course! I went to the funfair on Saturday with my brother and his girlfriend. I really like her. He has (2) _____ going out with her (3) _____ a few weeks now.

Tina: And what else?

Sarah: That night a strange old lady read my hand and predicted some really fantastic things.

Tina: Let me guess! You are (4) _____ to win the lottery.

Sarah: No, it's not that. I (5) _____ meet somebody very special soon who (6) _____ change my life!

Tina: Oh yes! And I suppose Leonardo DiCaprio is (7) _____ to fall in love with you! You should be ashamed of (8) _____ . You don't believe in all that rubbish, do you?

Sarah: Let's wait and see what happens.

4 Complete the sentences with the present perfect simple or continuous.

0 The couple *have invited* 50 people to their wedding. (invite)

1 I don't know this man. I _____ him before in my life. (never see)

2 They _____ away the plates. (not clear)

3 There is paper everywhere! The children _____ pictures for hours. (painting)

4 I _____ him three times today, but he was out. (ring)

5 _____ to your parents? (you ever lie)

6 He _____ all day and _____ a break for hours. (study, not have)

7 I know she _____ my favourite biscuits. I can smell them. (make)

5 Underline the correct answer.

0 How often do you go swimming? I **go/going** twice a week in the summer.

1 It's very important to believe in **yourself/you** if you want to be successful.

2 James has been living in France **for/since** 1998.

3 Sally **has finished/has been finishing** her book since last summer.

4 I really enjoyed **myself/me** at your party.

5 Paul has worked for that company **since/for** three years.

6 Complete the second sentence so that it means the same as the first one.

0 Drivers started using the new bridge in 1995. (since)
Drivers *have been using the new bridge since* 1995.

1 They met each other in 1998. (known)
They _____ since 1998.

2 She started learning French five years ago. (been)
She _____ for five years.

3 It's been a long time since I went to the cinema. (for)
I haven't _____ ages.

4 He started watching TV at 7pm. (since)
He _____ 7 pm.

LESSON 1 *They must be the islands!*

1 *must* and *can't* for deduction

We use **can't** to show we are sure something is not true.
We use **must** to show we are sure something is true.

For example, let's say your friend Martin has gone to Africa on safari until next month. Suddenly, you hear his voice outside your house!

You say – "That **can't** be Martin. He's in Africa. It **must** be someone else."

2 Past simple passive review

We form the **past simple passive** with the verb **be** in the past simple (was/were) and the **past participle** of the main verb.

We use the **past simple passive** to focus on the action, not the agent.
  The students **were given** a lot of homework by their teacher.
(We are more interested in how much homework the students had.)

  Maggie **was met** at the airport.
(We don't know who met her.)

The window **was broken**.
(We know Lenny broke it, but we don't want to get him into trouble)

The thief **was arrested**.
(It's obvious that the thief was arrested by the police.)

---

1 Match.

A		B
0 Listen to that noise! It	*d*	a. must be very upset.
1 The boy has lost his dog. He	☐	b. just won the lottery.
2 I heard John's voice. It	☐	c. you must be tired.
3 It must be incredibly expensive	☐	d. ~~must be rain falling on the roof.~~
4 He is not working this week so he	☐	e. must be him at the door.
5 If you fall asleep while you're watching TV,	☐	f. must be on holiday.
6 They can't be sad. They've	☐	g. to buy a boat.

2 Complete the sentences with *must* or *can't*.

0 She *must* love her dog very much. She takes him everywhere.

1 I don't believe it! It _____ be true.

2 Our teacher _____ be angry. She isn't smiling.

3 You _____ be keen on watersports. You hate getting wet.

4 That cat _____ hate fish. It never eats it.

5 The tourist _____ know the city well. He's never been here before.

3 Complete the sentences with *was* or *were*.

0   The house *was* destroyed in the fire.
1   Where _____ the shipwreck discovered?
2   The songs _____ sung beautifully by the children.
3   The tourists _____ flown by helicopter to the tropical island.
4   Who _____ the competition won by?
5   This painting _____ not painted by Picasso.
6   Many people _____ hurt when the train stopped suddenly.
7   The little boy _____ left all alone in the house.

4 Complete the sentences with the past simple passive.

0   He *was seen* at the scene of the crime. (see)
1   Dinner _____ before the guests arrived. (prepare)
2   This play _____ by Shakespeare. (write)
3   The new secretary _____ some letters to type. (give)
4   The children _____ to school by their parents. (take)
5   The pirates' treasure _____ never _____. (find)

5 Complete the sentences with the past simple passive. Use these verbs.

> buy ~~catch~~ hold make start take teach

0   The thief *was caught* by the police.
1   All the presents for the party _____ by my mum.
2   The fire _____ by accident.
3   The injured man _____ to hospital in an ambulance.
4   My new TV and video _____ in Japan.
5   The first Olympic Games _____ in Greece.
6   I _____ how to ski by a champion.

6 Complete the second sentence so that it means the same as the first one.

0   The police caught the thief.
    The thief *was caught* by the police.
1   Billy's mother woke him up at 8 o'clock.
    Billy _____ at 8 o'clock by his mother.
2   Someone broke a window yesterday at school.
    A window _____ yesterday at school.
3   A famous chef prepared the food for her birthday dinner.
    The food for her birthday dinner _____ by a famous chef.
4   My friend's parents drove me home after the party.
    I _____ home by my friend's parents after the party.
5   The boy took his dog for a walk every day.
    The dog _____ for a walk by the boy every day.

LESSON 2 *But the crab had gone*

1 Past perfect simple

We use the **past perfect simple** to describe the earlier of two actions.

We form the **past perfect simple** with the auxilary verb **have** in the **past** tense (**had**) and the **past participle** of the main verb.
They **had started** their homework before I went to their house.

Affirmative	Negative	Questions	Short answers
I had eaten	I hadn't eaten	Had I eaten?	Yes, I had./No, I hadn't.
you had eaten	you hadn't eaten	Had you eaten?	Yes, you had./No, you hadn't.
he had eaten	he hadn't eaten	Had he eaten?	Yes, he had./No, he hadn't.
she had eaten	she hadn't eaten	Had she eaten?	Yes, she had./No, she hadn't.
it had eaten	it hadn't eaten	Had it eaten?	Yes, it had./No, it hadn't.
we had eaten	we hadn't eaten	Had we eaten?	Yes, we had./No, we hadn't.
you had eaten	you hadn't eaten	Had you eaten?	Yes, you had./No, you hadn't.
they had eaten	they hadn't eaten	Had they eaten?	Yes, they had./No, they hadn't.

2 Past perfect simple and past simple

How do we decide which of these two past tenses to use? We've already said we use the **past perfect simple** for actions that happened **before** other actions that happened in the past.

So if we ate a pizza at 6 o'clock last night and we watched TV at 9 o'clock last night, we would say –
    We **had eaten** a pizza when we **watched** TV.
We ate the pizza first, so we use the **past perfect simple** for that action.
We watched TV after, so we use the **past simple** for that action.

If you arrived at school at half past nine and the lessons started at nine o'clock, you would say:
    When I **arrived** at school, the lessons **had started**.

---

1 Complete the sentences with the past perfect.

0   It was the first time she *had seen* a play at the theatre. (see)

1   George _____ his homework when his friend came round. (do)

2   Fortunately Wendy _____ the house before I got there. (not leave)

3   She was happy because she was given the CD she _____ for. (asked)

4   When I _____ my shopping, I had lunch in a café. (finish)

5   Until she smiled, he _____ how beautiful she was. (not notice)

6   Helen phoned him but he _____ out for the day. (go)

2 Write questions and short answers about what you had and hadn't done before you went to school yesterday.

0   have breakfast
     Had you had breakfast? Yes, I had.

1   brush your hair
     _____ _____

2   do your homework
     _____ _____

3   take the dog for a walk
     _____ _____

4   clean your teeth
     _____ _____

5   pack your school bag
     _____ _____

3 **When Mum and Dad came home, the house was in a terrible mess. Write sentences saying what Jenny and Simon *had* and *hadn't done.***

0 Jenny/not do washing up

Jenny hadn't done the washing up.

1 Simon/not tidy up his bedroom

_____

2 Jenny/break a glass

_____

3 Jenny/leave her dirty clothes on floor

_____

4 Simon/not take the rubbish out

_____

5 Simon and Jenny/not make their beds

_____

6 Simon and his friends/drop chocolate ice cream on the sofa

_____

4 **Join the sentences using *after* + the past perfect.**

0 We had lunch. Then we went out to play.

We went out *to play after we had had lunch.*

1 The bus left. Then we arrived at the bus stop.

We arrived _____

2 The people left the building. Then the bomb exploded.

The bomb exploded _____

3 She was ill. Then she met Tom.

She _____

4 He played football. Then he had a shower.

He had _____

5 She went to the bank. Then she bought a present.

She bought _____

5 **Complete the sentences with the past perfect and past simple.**

0 The thief had *left* before anyone *noticed* the diamond was missing. (leave, notice)

1 I _____ the test before the teacher _____ for the exam papers back. (finish, ask)

2 I _____ of the place she _____ it. (not hear, describe)

3 When my grandmother first _____ in the city, she _____ a car. (arrive, never see)

4 When I _____ to him, he _____ breakfast. (spoke, not have)

5 They _____ to the theatre because they _____ the tickets. (not go, lost)

6 I panicked because it _____ the day before Christmas and I _____ any shopping. (be, not do)

7 The children who _____ to the farm _____ a horse before. (go, not ride)

8 The film star _____ by the time the reporter _____ . (leave, arrive)

LESSON 3 *He had been telling the truth!*

Past perfect continuous

The **past perfect continuous** belongs to the **continuous** family of tenses, so there are some things you know about it already:

- it uses the auxiliary verb **be** – this time in the **past perfect** tense (**had been**);
- the main verb has the ending **–ing**;
- it tells us about something that **continued** in the past.

Affirmative	Negative	Questions	Short answers
I had been running	I hadn't been running	Had I been running?	Yes, I had./No, I hadn't.
you had been running	you hadn't been running	Had you been running?	Yes, you had./No, you hadn't.
he had been running	he hadn't been running	Had he been running?	Yes, he had./No, he hadn't.
she had been running	she hadn't been running	Had she been running?	Yes, she had./No, she hadn't.
it had been running	it hadn't been running	Had it been running?	Yes, it had./No, it hadn't.
we had been running	we hadn't been running	Had we been running?	Yes, we had./No, we hadn't.
you had been running	you hadn't been running	Had you been running?	Yes, you had./No, you hadn't.
they had been running	they hadn't been running	Had they been running?	Yes, they had./No, they hadn't.

The **past perfect continuous** is another tense that goes with the **past simple**.

> I **had been cleaning** all afternoon, so when you **came** back I was tired.
> She **had been reading** for hours when her friend **phoned**.

When do we use the **past perfect continuous**? We use it for an activity over a period before another past action.

> The sun **had been shining** for half an hour when it **started** to rain.
> He was hot because he **had been dancing** all evening.

1 Complete the sentences with the past perfect continuous.

0 They *had been playing* music loudly all evening before anyone complained. (play)

1 He _____ for hours so I decided to wake him up. (sleep)

2 We _____ all day when the ship finally appeared. (wait)

3 A strong wind _____ all night. It did a lot of damage. (blow)

4 We realized later that the little boy _____ the truth. (tell)

5 _____ the rescuers _____ for the climber in the wrong place? (look)

6 The pirate ship _____ stolen treasure when it sank. (carry)

7 He was tired because he _____ all morning. (windsurf)

2 Complete the sentences with the past perfect simple or continuous form of these verbs.

crash	~~decide~~ destroy eat miss play rain

0 She hadn't finished her homework, but she *decided* to go out anyway.

1 When the city flooded, it _____ for days.

2 The band _____ together for years before they became famous.

3 I had trusted him with my car, but he _____ it anyway.

4 I wasn't hungry because I _____ before the party.

5 When the children went back to the beach, the waves _____ the sandcastle.

6 Johnny was late for work again because he _____ the bus.

3 Write questions and answers.

0 Grace was hot and tired. (run/dance)

Had she been running? No, she had been dancing.

1 Tim's hands were black and dirty. (paint the garage/fix the car)

_____

2 George felt sick. (eat a lot of cakes/drink a lot of cola)

_____

3 Luke's eyes were red. (cry/study all night)

_____

4 Sally's hair was wet. (walk in rain/swim)

_____

5 Laura and Mary were laughing loudly. (watch cartoons/tell jokes)

_____

4 Complete the sentences with the past perfect continuous and past simple.

0 A shark *had been swimming* round and round the divers for a long time before they *noticed* it. (swim, notice)

1 He _____ on the bus for half an hour when he _____ it was going the wrong way. (sit, realise)

2 The detective _____ the thief for a month before he finally _____ him. (follow, catch)

3 The teacher _____ Bill's mother because he _____ a lot of lessons. (ring, miss)

4 They _____ money for many years before they _____ married. (save, get)

5 He _____ English for years before he _____ the exam. (study, pass)

5 Complete the text with the past simple or past perfect continuous. Use these verbs.

not have   not need   realise   sit   sleep   think   turn on   use   want   work   ~~work~~

Sam Tompson was a brilliant young inventor who (0) *had been working* on a secret project for a couple of years. She (1) _____ to invent a mobile phone that (2) _____ batteries! Batteries needed electricity to make them work and that meant that it was impossible to go on a long journey to somewhere that (3) _____ electricity. But what else could she use?

Sam (4) _____ about this for some time, when suddenly one hot day she had an amazing idea. The sun! Why couldn't she use power from the sun? People (5) _____ the sun's energy for years, so why not use it for her phone, too?

Sam (6) _____ down in front of her computer and started to design the new phone. The hours passed and at 6 o'clock she (7) _____ that she (8) _____ all night. She turned off the computer and went home, thinking about how famous she was going to be.

She (9) _____ for only a few hours when the phone rang. She picked it up.

'Hello, is that Sam Tompson? This is the Police,' a voice said. 'I'm sorry, but there has been a break-in at your office.' 'Oh, no!' Sam said. 'I'll be there in five minutes.'

When she arrived at her office, everything looked normal. Nothing was missing. Nothing had been broken. The police left and Sam sat down to work. She (10) _____ her computer and then she realised what had happened. The computer was empty. Someone had stolen her design!

3 TREASURE!

LESSON 4 — *Use Your Grammar*

❶ The past

You now know all these **past tenses**:
past simple
past continuous
past perfect simple
past perfect continuous
past simple passive

We use the **past simple** to talk about actions that started and finished in the past – and we know the exact time when they happened.
　　We **arrived** at the hotel on Monday morning.

We use the **past continuous** for actions that happened in the past, when we want to emphasise the fact that they continued for a period of time.
　　We **were walking** down the street when we heard those strange noises again.

We use the **past perfect simple** to talk about actions that happened in the past **before** other past actions.
　　When we got to the station, the train **had gone.**

We use the **present perfect continuous** for actions that had continued in the past **before** other past actions.
　　We **had been walking** all day when we got to the hotel.

We use the **past simple passive** to emphasise the action rather than the agent.
　　We **were hurt** when the car crashed.

❷ Don't forget!

You can make your writing more interesting by joining sentences together – **although** and **but** are **connecting words** which to help you do this.
　　Although it was raining, we had a picnic in the forest.
　　It was raining, **but** we had a picnic in the forest.

---

1 Complete the sentences using your own ideas. Use the tense in brackets at the end of each sentence.

1　Yesterday, two people _____. (past simple)

2　They had _____. (past perfect simple)

3　She had _____.
　　(past perfect continuous)

4　The cake _____. (past simple passive)

5　The boy didn't _____. (past simple)

6　We were _____. (past continuous)

7　My book _____. (past simple passive)

8　Peter was _____. (past continuous)

9　I had _____.
　　(past perfect continuous)

10　It had _____.
　　(past perfect simple)

2 Answer these questions about yourself. Use complete sentences.

1　What were you doing before this lesson?

　　_____

2　Was your bag stolen last week?

　　_____

3　What did you do last night?

　　_____

4　What were you doing at eight o'clock yesterday morning?

　　_____

5　Had you eaten a sandwich before this lesson started?

　　_____

6　Did you watch TV this morning?

　　_____

3 Complete the text with the verbs in the correct tense.

Last night my Grandfather John (0) *told* (tell) me a story about what happened one day when he was a boy.
His family (1) _____ (live) in a big house in a village. They were rich and they (2) _____
(have) servants. One of these was a boy called George who (3) _____ (work) in the garden at that time.
George and John were the same age and they (4) _____ (be) best friends ever since George
(5) _____ (come) to work in the village. In those days it wasn't normal for rich boys to be friends with
the servants.

One weekend John and one of his friends (6) _____ (decide) to go hunting in the forest near the
village. They were too young, really, to go by themselves, but they (7) _____ (go) anyway.
They (8) _____ (not tell) anyone where they were going or when they would be back. Only George
(9) _____ (know) and he (10) _____ (promise) not to tell.

The day passed and it (11) _____ (get) dark. George expected to hear John and his friend laughing and
joking any moment, but it got later and later and by nine o clock they still (12) _____ (not come) back.
George was really worried and finally he (13) _____ (decide) to go and look for them. He couldn't tell
anyone what (14) _____ (happen) but he had to do something. He got his knife, put some bread and
cheese in a bag and (15) _____ (walk) into the forest.

4 What do you think happened next? Finish the story.

_____
_____
_____
_____
_____
_____
_____
_____
_____
_____
_____
_____
_____
_____
_____

3 TREASURE!

LESSON 5 *Test Yourself*

1 **Complete the sentences with *must* or *can't*.**

0   Lucy *can't* be late for work. It's not like her.

1   The girl _____ be very upset. She had an argument with her best friend.

2   It _____ be a very difficult question. Nobody can answer it.

3   That dog looks dangerous. It _____ be friendly.

4   You _____ be serious about leaving school. That's a big mistake.

5   They helped me a lot. They _____ be nice people.

2 **Complete the sentences with the past simple or past perfect simple.**

0   The waiters *had cleared* away the plates when the bill *arrived*. (clear, arrive)

1   James _____ in a small village where he _____ school. (live, start)

2   Last night the children all _____ for the party. (dress up)

3   He _____ out to a fast food restaurant with his friends last night. (go)

4   She _____ the news when I _____ her last week. (not hear, see)

5   He couldn't see properly because he _____ his glasses the day before. (break)

6   Sarah _____ to invite you to her party a few minutes ago. (call)

7   The thief _____ before the police _____. (escape, arrive)

8   We _____ for a while before we noticed that the bus _____ . (chat, go)

9   The two friends _____ contact for a while but then they _____ in touch again. (lose, get)

10 I _____ the whole family together since my sister _____ married. (not see, get)

3 **Rewrite the sentences in the passive.**

0   The secretary lost all the papers.
    All the papers were lost by the secretary.

1   The bad weather spoiled our picnic.

    _____

2   Mark carefully tied up the canoe.

    _____

3   A famous architect designed this castle.

    _____

4   The people gave the president a special welcome.

    _____

5   Her mother made her wedding dress.

    _____

34

4 Complete the text with the correct answers.

It was Christmas Eve. All the family was together for the holiday. The younger children
(0) *had gone* to bed. They were very tired because they (1) _____ outside in the snow
all day.

I (2) _____ in my armchair, listening to everyone laughing and talking.
'Wake up, Father!' someone (3) _____ . 'We're going to tell ghost stories!'
The lights (4) _____ off. Suddenly the room was dark. I smiled as I listened to the young
people. The stories were full of horror, but I (5) _____ by them. They were not true.

I (6) _____ to them for some time when I remembered some things which were terrible
because they were true! 'Tell us a ghost story, Father!' someone shouted. 'You (7) _____
know some ghost stories!'

I (8) _____ up, cold and shaking. 'No! No!' I shouted, 'I have no stories to tell!'
I hurried from the room, away from them all and went out into the garden. I stood there in the
cold. My heart was beating (9) _____ . I (10) _____ with fear. Will I never forget?
Will I never find peace?

0	a. <u>had been</u>	b. were gone	c. were being
1	a. played	b. are playing	c. had been playing
2	a. had sat	b. sat	c. sit
3	a. did shout	b. shouted	c. shouting
4	a. have turned	b. are turned	c. were turned
5	a. wasn't scared	b. didn't scared	c. scared
6	a. listened	b. had been listening	c. wasn't listening
7	a. can't	b. mustn't	c. must
8	a. stood	b. was standing	c. have stood
9	a. fastly	b. fastest	c. fast
10	a. had been shaking	b. was shaking	c. did shake

If you would like to find out what happens in this story,
read *The Woman In Black* by Susan Hill. Macmillan Guided Readers Elementary Level.

LESSON 1 *He's such an idiot!*

1 *What ...!*

We use **What ...!** to make an exclamation.
> **What** a lovely house!
> **What** beautiful flowers!
> **What** an ugly picture!

Top Tip!

Don't forget to put an exclamation mark (!) at the end of the sentence.

2 *So/such*

We use **so** and **such** when we want to add emphasis to adjectives and adverbs.
We use **so** with adjectives not accompanied by a noun, and with adverbs.
> That house is **so** lovely!
> Our dog runs **so** quickly!

We use **such** (a/an) with adjectives accompanied by a noun.
> That is **such** a lovely house!
> Our dog is **such** a fast runner!

3 Result clauses

We use **so/such** ... to express result.
We form result clauses with **so** + adjective/adverb + (that) or **such** (a/an) + adjective + noun + (that).

We often leave out 'that', especially in spoken English.
> He was **so** tall (**that**) he could reach the ceiling.
> It was **such** a lovely day (**that**) we decided to go swimming.

1 Complete the sentences with *so* or *such*.

0 He never takes a break. He is *so* busy.

1 Lassie can do amazing tricks. She is _____ a clever dog.

2 We read a true story about pirates and treasure. It was _____ exciting.

3 We went to Cornwall this summer. It was _____ a fabulous holiday.

4 Have you seen Sarah swimming? She's _____ fast.

5 Can you help me carry this? It's _____ a heavy bag.

6 I really enjoyed that lesson. It was _____ interesting.

7 The students couldn't do the maths test. It was _____ difficult.

8 Jim makes friends easily. He's _____ a friendly person.

2 Now rewrite your answers from exercise 1 using *What ...!*

0 What *a busy man he is!*

1 What _____

2 What _____

3 What _____

4 What _____

5 What _____

6 What _____

7 What _____

8 What _____

3 Join the sentences using *so/such... that*.

0 He was badly injured. He was taken to hospital.
He was so badly injured that he was taken to hospital.

1 The actor was very nervous. He forgot his lines.
_____

2 It was a cold day. We were all shivering.
_____

3 He had a very tiring day. He fell asleep on the bus.
_____

4 He was driving fast. The car went out of control.
_____

5 The food tasted terrible. They couldn't eat it.
_____

6 The Scottish islands are very beautiful. They are visited by many tourists.
_____

7 Vicky is a very lazy girl. She never helps at home.
_____

4 Complete the second sentence so that it means the same as the first one.

0 He's a slow learner and it takes him ages to do his homework. (that)
He's *such a slow learner that* it takes him ages to do his homework.

1 Michael is such a good tennis player. (so)
Michael _____ well.

2 Dolphins swim so fast. (such)
Dolphins are _____ swimmers.

3 He drove very dangerously and he had an accident. (that)
He _____ he had an accident.

4 It was very dark and we couldn't see anything. (so)
It was _____ we couldn't see anything.

5 He ate a lot of cakes and felt sick. (that)
He ate _____ he felt sick.

5 Complete the sentences. Use your imagination.

1 It was so cold that _____

2 It was such a hot day that _____

3 My mother was so proud of me that _____

4 I was so angry that _____

5 It was such an easy test that _____

6 She told so many lies that _____

7 They are such a rich family that _____

8 My father is so busy that _____

4 ADVENTURE

Whales have been hunted ...

❶ Present continuous passive

We form the **present continuous passive** with the verb **be** in the **present continuous** tense (am being, are being, is being), and the **past participle** of the main verb.

Affirmative	Negative	Questions
I am being met at the airport.	I am not being ...	Am I being ...?
You are being met at the airport.	You are not being ...	Are you being ...?
He is being met at the airport.	He isn't being ...	Is he being ...?
She is being met at the airport.	She isn't being ...	Is she being ...?
It is being met at the airport.	It isn't being ...	Is it being ...?
We are being met at the airport.	We aren't being ...	Are we being ...?
You are being met at the airport.	You aren't being ...	Are you being ...?
They are being met at the airport.	They aren't being ...	Are they being ...?

As with all passive tenses, we use the present continuous passive to focus on the action rather than the agent.

Our dog **is being examined** right now.

They are **being taken** to a top restaurant for dinner.

❷ Present perfect passive

We form the **present perfect passive** with the verb **be** in the **present perfect** tense (have been, has been) and the **past participle** of the main verb.

Affirmative	Negative	Questions
I have been photographed	I haven't been photographed	Have I been photographed?
you have been photographed	you haven't been photographed	Have you been photographed?
he has been photographed	he has been photographed	Has he been photographed?
she has been photographed	she hasn't been photographed	Has she been photographed?
it has been photographed	it hasn't been photographed	Has it been photographed?
we have been photographed	we haven't been photographed	Have we been photographed?
you have been photographed	you haven't been photographed	Have you been photographed?
they have been photographed	they haven't been photographed	Have they been photographed?

As with all the passive tenses, we use the **present perfect passive** to focus on the action and not the agent.

My sister **has been taken** to hospital.

Many whales **have been killed** this year.

❶ Complete the sentences with the present continuous passive.

0 The new airport *is being built*. (build)

1 The class _____ by the headteacher today. (teach)

2 The plants _____ by the gardener. (water)

3 The school _____ . (paint)

4 The actors _____ a lot of money for this film. (pay)

5 The athletes _____ for the Olympics. (prepare)

2 **Now rewrite the sentences in exercise 1 as questions.**

0   *Is the new airport being built?*

1   _____

2   _____

3   _____

4   _____

5   _____

3 **Emily is having a party. Write what *has* and *hasn't been done.***

–	send invitations	✓	0	*The invitations have been sent.*
–	make cake	✗	1	_____
–	order sandwiches	✓	2	_____
–	choose music	✗	3	_____
–	put up balloons	✗	4	_____
–	buy going-home presents	✓	5	_____

4 **Complete the sentences with the present perfect passive or present continuous passive.**

0   Has your dog *been found* yet? (find)

1   The police are here because the house _____ . (break into)

2   The children _____ by the babysitter at the moment. (look after)

3   The old car _____ because it won't start. (push)

4   The bank robber _____ yet. (not catch)

5   The rubbish _____ and it smells terrible. (burn)

5 **Complete the second sentence so that it means the same as the first one.**

0   I have told you a hundred times not to shout in class.
    You *have been told a hundred times* not to shout in class.

1   Millions of tourists have visited the Pyramids in Egypt.
    The Pyramids in Egypt _____ of tourists.

2   A vet is examining the sick animals.
    The sick animals _____ a vet.

3   Police have warned drivers not to use this road.
    Drivers _____ not to use this road.

4   The workmen are making a special path for bicycles.
    A special path _____ for bicycles.

5   The zookeepers are feeding the animals.
    The animals _____ the zookeepers.

4 ADVENTURE

LESSON 3 *You won't be attacked!*

---

1 Future passive

We form the **future passive** with the verb **be** in the **future tense** (will be) and the **past participle** of the main verb.

Affirmative	Negative	Question
I will be given	I won't be given	Will I be given?
you will be given	you won't be given	Will you be given?
he will be given	he won't be given	Will he be given?
she will be given	she won't be given	Will she be given?
it will be given	it won't be given	Will it be given?
we will be given	we won't be given	Will we be given?
you will be given	you won't be given	Will you be given?
they will be given	they won't be given	Will they be given?

We use the **future passive** like we use the **future active** – to talk about things that we hope or predict will happen in the future. Because it is the **passive** voice, we use it to focus on the action rather than the agent.

We **will be met** by Sharon.

You **won't be given** extra homework this week.

Will I be told about the new job?

---

1 Complete the sentences with the future passive.

0 The winners of the competition *will be taken* on a cruise to the Caribbean. (take)

1 The divers hope treasure _____ in the shipwreck. (find)

2 _____ all your holiday _____ in one place? (spend)

3 Keep still and you _____ by the dog. (not attack)

4 _____ all your friends _____ to your party? (invite)

5 The house _____ next year. (sell)

6 Housework _____ by robots in the future. (do)

7 New planets _____ . (discover)

8 The film _____ by a famous director. (make)

9 You _____ for the school play if you can't sing and dance. (not choose)

10 The competition _____ by the best team. (win)

40

2 **Complete the sentences with *will* or *will be*.**

0   Students *will be* taught French and German next year.

1   The children promise they _____ look after the dog.

2   The match _____ played at the stadium on Sunday.

3   Your car _____ kept in a garage while you're away.

4   The couple _____ borrow money from the bank to buy a house.

5   The student _____ allowed to leave early because he's ill.

6   The weather forecast says it _____ rain tomorrow.

7   The tourists _____ taken to see the city's sights by the tour guide.

8   The furniture _____ moved to make room for dancing.

9   The pizza _____ delivered at 8 o'clock.

10 We _____ finish this exercise tomorrow.

3 **Look at the timetable for a school trip and write sentences in the future passive. Do not use the agent + *by*.**

09.00 pick up children from school

09.30 drive to museum

10.00 teacher tells children about museum

12.00 teacher shows children around museum

13.00 teacher gives children sandwiches

14.00 take children back to school

0   *The children will be picked up from school at nine o'clock.*

1   _____

2   _____

3   _____

4   _____

5   _____

4 **Complete the text with the future passive.**

Come to Jamaica for the experience of a lifetime! You (0) *will be* (be) amazed by the beautiful beaches and the clear blue sea. When you arrive at the airport you (1) _____ (meet) by our driver and you (2) _____ (take) to the ship. On board you (3) _____ (show) to your luxurious cabin where you can rest and unpack. At 8 o'clock in the evening you (4) _____ (invite) to a Welcome Dinner with the Captain and crew.

During your cruise you can play tennis, watch a film, go swimming or simply relax in the sun. The rest of your trip will be spent visiting the islands of the Caribbean and enjoying youself.

All meals and entertainment (5) _____ (include) in the price of the holiday.

LESSON 4 *Use Your Grammar*

❶ Passive voice

You now know five tenses in the **passive voice**:
Present simple – with am/is/are
Present continuous – with am being/is being/are being
Present perfect – with have been/has been
Past simple – with was/were
Past continuous – with was being/were being

To include the agent in the **passive voice** we use the word **by** + the agent.
   The building was designed **by** a famous architect.

❷ *What …!*

When we want to emphasise our enthusiasm or amazement about something we are describing or writing about, we can use **What …!** The exclamation mark (!) at the end of the sentence also emphasises our feelings/opinion.
   What a brilliant film!

Don't forget, you can use **so** and **such** for emphasis too.
   It was **such** a great film that I went to see it three times.

❸ Connecting words and phrases

Connecting words and phrases are important because they can help you to join ideas.

We use **either … or …** when we are talking about a choice between two situations or things.
   She will study **either** dancing **or** acting.

We use **both … and …** when we are talking about two things together (i.e. not a choice between two things).
   They like **both** skating **and** skiing.

1 Complete the text with the correct passive tense of the verbs in brackets.

A new shopping centre (1) _____ (build) a new shopping centre in our town at the moment. It (2) _____ (made) out of glass and metal and will look very modern when it's finished. Work on the centre (3) _____ (go on) for three months now. The building that was there before (4) _____ (knock) down just before the work started. The new shopping centre (5) _____ (expect) to open for business in three months time. Everybody in town (6) just _____ (send) an invitation to go and visit the new centre when it is finished.

2 Complete the sentences using your imagination.

1   It was such a fantastic day that _____ .
2   Sandy is going to study either _____ .
3   The students were being _____ .
4   I love both _____ .
5   My clothes have been _____ .

3 Choose the correct word.

1 Our school has been _____ and now it looks extremely nice.

   a. paints   b. painting   c. painted

2 It was _____ a terrible book that I couldn't read it.

   a. so   b. such   c. very

3 The flowers _____ when I visited the garden centre.

   a. were being watered   b. was being watered   c. were been watered

4 I think we're having _____ pizza or spaghetti for dinner tonight.

   a. both   b. or   c. either

5 _____ a beautiful dog!

   a. That   b. What   c. So

6 I _____ on my English grammar at the moment!

   a. was being tested   b. have been tested   c. am being tested

4 Sarah sent this e-mail to a friend.
Read the text and then complete it using the notes below and your imagination.

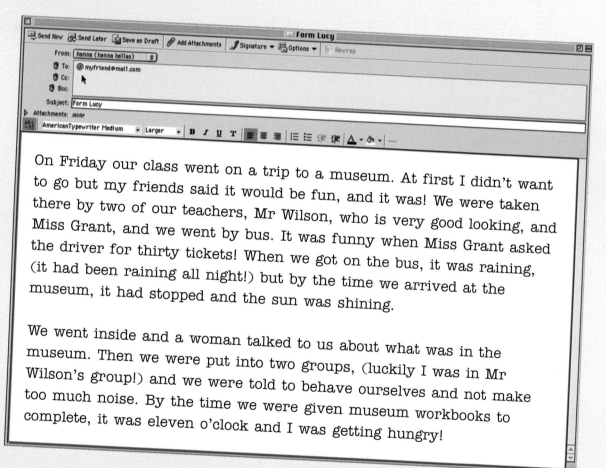

On Friday our class went on a trip to a museum. At first I didn't want to go but my friends said it would be fun, and it was! We were taken there by two of our teachers, Mr Wilson, who is very good looking, and Miss Grant, and we went by bus. It was funny when Miss Grant asked the driver for thirty tickets! When we got on the bus, it was raining, (it had been raining all night!) but by the time we arrived at the museum, it had stopped and the sun was shining.

We went inside and a woman talked to us about what was in the museum. Then we were put into two groups, (luckily I was in Mr Wilson's group!) and we were told to behave ourselves and not make too much noise. By the time we were given museum workbooks to complete, it was eleven o'clock and I was getting hungry!

too early for lunch	lunch in the museum restaurant
so hungry that ...	good food – spaghetti, chips, pizza, ice cream
Egyptian mummies	walk in park – sunny, not cold
model of an ancient village	bus back to school
treasure from a shipwreck	museum workbook for homework

Test Yourself

1 Join the sentences with *so/such a/an* and *that*.

0   It was a very hot day. I didn't want to go out.
It was such a hot day that I didn't want to go out.

1   He behaves badly. Nobody likes him.
_____

2   Dolphins are friendly animals. You can swim with them.
_____

3   The dog ate too much. It couldn't move.
_____

4   It was a boring film. We left in the middle of it.
_____

5   The students are excited about the trip. They can't sit still.
_____

2 Complete the sentences with *so* or *such* and your own words.

0   I'm *so* hungry that I could eat all day.
1   Our teacher was _____ angry _____
2   He's always _____ grumpy that _____
3   He is _____ a lazy person that _____
4   Mother is _____ busy that _____
5   It's _____ a lovely day that _____
6   We had _____ a fabulous time at the zoo that _____
7   My brother is _____ an idiot that _____

3 Complete the sentences with *be, being* or *been.*

0   Mark hasn't *been* well for the last few days.
1   Will wildlife _____ protected in the future?
2   I can't use my computer because the electricity has _____ cut off.
3   There will _____ trouble when your parents see your report card.
4   The mountains have _____ covered in snow since last night.
5   Many shipwrecks are _____ discovered near the island.
6   We won't _____ late for school tomorrow.
7   I'll take the bus because my car is _____ repaired.
8   The injured people are _____ taken to hospital in an ambulance.
9   She is _____ trained for the school basketball team.
10 There has _____ a lot of rain recently.

4   Rewrite the sentences in the passive.

0   We have spent a lot of money on computers.
A lot of money has been spent on computers.

1   Someone will answer the phone.

_____

2   They are buying new equipment for the office.

_____

3   Is someone reading a story to the children?

_____

4   Has someone stolen the valuable painting?

_____

5   They won't finish the work until next week.

_____

5   Underline the correct answer.

0   I'm scared because I'm _____ followed by a dog.
  a. be   b. being   c. been

1   It was _____ cold that the lake had frozen.
  a. such a   b. such   c. so

2   Sarah has _____ underwater for a long time.
  a. being   b. been   c. be

3   The room _____ tidied up by my brother at the moment.
  a. will be   b. has been   c. is being

4   The results of the exam _____ known in a few days.
  a. have been   b. will be   c. are being

5   It was _____ easy test that all the students passed it.
  a. so an   b. such   c. such an

6   Meals and hotels _____ included in the price of the holiday.
  a. will   b. are being   c. will be

7   It's _____ such a long time since I last saw you.
  a. being   b. been   c. be

8   She speaks English _____ that you think she's from England.
  a. such good   b. so good   c. so well

9   He was _____ surprised that he couldn't speak.
  a. such a   b. so   c. very

10   My favourite singer _____ interviewed on MTV now.
  a. has been   b. will   c. is being

LESSON 1 *She said she was really upset*

Reported statements

We use **reported statements** to report what somebody said in the past. We only use **past tenses** in **reported statements**.

We don't use speech marks (") in **reported statements**. We only use those when we are writing the exact words that somebody is saying (direct speech). Instead, we use the **reporting verbs said** or **told**.

"I like your dress."
Lisa **said** (that) she **liked my dress**.
but Lisa **told** me (that) she **liked my class**.

Note that **tell** is always followed by the object: we tell somebody something.

Direct speech	Reported statements
Present simple	Past simple
Present continuous	Past continuous
Present perfect	Past perfect simple
Past simple	Past perfect

"I am going to the cinema."
Larry said he was going to the cinema.

"It was a great party."
Tim said it had been a great party.

Direct speech	Reported statements
am/is/are	was/were
have/has	had
do/does	did
will	would
can	could

"I will wash the dishes."
Dad said he would wash the dishes.

"It is my birthday."
Holly said it was her birthday.

We also change personal pronouns and possessive pronouns in reported statements:

I ➔ he/she
we ➔ they
my ➔ his/her
our ➔ their

We change adverbials of **time** and **place** when we **report statements**.

now	**then**
today	**that day**
ago	**before**
yesterday	**the previous day**
last (week)	**the (week) before/ the previous (week)**
tomorrow	**the following day**
next (week)	**the following (week)**
this	**that – the**
here	**there**

"I'm watching TV this evening."
He said he was watching **that** evening.

"This is the book I want."
He said that was the book he wanted.

Note that when something is reported that is still true the tense need not change.
'Turkey is a great place for a holiday.'
She said Turkey **is** a great place for a holiday.

1 **Complete the second sentence so that it means the same as the first one.**

0   'I don't like getting up early in the morning,' said Jane.   Jane said she *didn't like getting up* early in the morning.

1   'I don't believe in ghosts,' said Nick.   Nick said he _____ in ghosts.

2   'I've eaten too much,' complained Anne.   Anne complained that she _____ too much.

3   'We didn't mean to laugh,' they told their teacher.   They told their teacher they _____ to laugh.

4   'I can finish my homework later,' said Rachel.   Rachel said she _____ her homework later.

2 **Rewrite the dialogue in reported speech.**

0   **Miss Evans:** My students are very noisy today.
1   **Mr Brown:**   They are excited about the holiday tomorrow.
2   **Miss Evans:** Yes, I can't wait for the holiday!
3   **Mr Brown:**   I know how you feel.
4   **Miss Evans:** I've given my class a lot of homework this week.
5   **Mr Brown:**   I am not giving them much to do for the holiday.
6   **Miss Evans:** That will make them happy.

0   *Miss Evans said her students were very noisy that day.*
1   _____
2   _____
3   _____
4   _____
5   _____
6   _____

3 **Complete the sentences with the correct form of** *see, hear, feel* **and** *watch*.

0   She *watched* the artist painting a beautiful picture.
1   She _____ something touching her face in the dark and screamed.
2   It can't be Mike at the door. I _____ him leaving 2 hours ago.
3   We stood at the door and _____ the car driving away.
4   I can _____ footsteps coming up the path to the house. It must be the postman.

4 **Join the sentences.**

0   I can hear my father. He is singing in the shower.
    I can hear my father singing in the shower.
1   The babysitter watched the children. They were playing in the garden.
    The babysitter _____
2   The two cars were crashing. Lucy saw them.
    Lucy _____
3   The sun is shining. I can feel it on my back.
    I _____
4   Nick was winning the race. She saw him.
    She _____

LESSON 2 *She asked if ACE was haunted*

Reported questions

In **reported questions** we use the affirmative form of the verb and we don't use a question mark.

We use special **reporting verbs:** for example **asked** and **wanted to know**.
   "What time is it?"
She **asked** me what time it was.

We change the tense in exactly the same way as we do when we **report statements**.

● Reported *yes/no* questions: we use **if** after **asked**.
   The subject comes after **if** and before the verb.
      "Are you tired?"
   She asked me **if** I was tired.

● Reported *wh–* questions:
   The subject comes after the *wh–* word and before the verb.

"**When** are you leaving?"
   Are you leaving?"
She asked me **when** I was leaving.

"**Why** did you go there?"
He wanted to know **why** I had gone there.

Note that we can't say "She asked me when was I leaving". Word order in reported questions is the same as reported statements.

Remember –
We change the pronouns in **reported questions** just like in **reported statements**.

---

1 Rewrite these questions in reported speech.

0   'Did you remember to bring your keys?'
   He asked her *if she had remembered to bring her keys.*

1   'Do you come from the USA?'
   She asked him _____

2   'What's the time?'
   She wanted to know _____

3   'Is Tom coming to the party?'
   She asked _____

4   'Are they having dinner?'
   She wanted to know _____

5   'Have you ever visited a foreign country?'
   She asked him _____

6   'Did Jake see a famous film star in the street?'
   She asked _____

2 Rewrite these questions in reported speech.

0   'Where have you been all day?'
   My mother asked me *where I had been all day.*

1   'What are you doing at the moment?'
   He asked me _____

2   'Where will you be tomorrow?'
   He wanted to know _____

3   'How long have you known your best friend?'
   He asked me _____

4   'What did you forget to bring?'
   He asked _____

5   'Who does the sports car belong to?'
   He asked me _____

6   'Where can I buy cheap clothes?'
   He wanted to know _____

3 **Sarah is new at school and is asking Tom these questions. Complete the sentences with reported speech.**

0 'What's your name?'
Sarah asked Tom *what his name was.*

1 'What's our teacher's name?'
She asked Tom _____

2 'Does he give his class a lot of homework?'
She wanted to know _____

3 'Is there a computer room in the school?'
She asked Tom _____

4 'Do we go on day trips to interesting places?'
She asked him _____

5 'What sports can we play?'
She asked Tom _____

6 'Did you walk to school or did you catch the bus?'
She wanted to know _____

7 'Have you been at the school long?'
She asked him _____

8 'Am I going to like my new school?'
She wanted to know _____

9 'Where is our classroom?'
She wanted to know _____

10 'Have you got a girlfriend?'
She asked Tom _____

4 **Write these questions in direct speech.**

0 Tom asked me if I had got a new bike.
"Have you got a new bike?"

1 He wanted to know why I couldn't finish my homework.
_____

2 Jane asked them if they knew where the new book shop was.
_____

3 She asked who the strange man with red hair was.
_____

4 Mum asked me if I was going to buy some new clothes for the party.
_____

5 He asked me what I wanted to be when I grew up.
_____

6 Fred asked her if she would make him a sandwich.
_____

7 She asked me if I had ever been to Venice.
_____

8 He wanted to know why I hadn't tidied my room.
_____

5 **Put the words in the right order to make questions. Ask a friend and then write their answers in reported speech.**

0 you maths like do
Do you like maths?

Sally said she liked maths.

1 go did yesterday out you?
_____

_____

2 play you can tennis?
_____

_____

3 my help will with me homework you?
_____

_____

4 you England been have to ever?
_____

_____

5 book lend you me will your?
_____

_____

6 like you Ricky Martin do?
_____

_____

LESSON 3 *She used to frighten the family*

Used to …

We can use **used to** when we talk about past habits and states.
After **used to** we use the **infinitive** of the main verb – without **to**.

> **I used to** go to the beach every summer.

(But now I don't go to the beach every summer.)

We make questions with **used to** like this – **Did you use to** go out often when you were young?
We make **negatives** with **used to** like this – We **didn't use to** go abroad a few years ago.

Be careful!
When you use **used to** for questions or negatives you change it to **use to**.

> **Top Tip!**
>
> For present habits and states we use the present simple:
> **She walks**. (NOT she **uses to walk**.)

---

1 **Underline the mistakes and rewrite the sentences correctly.**

0 We <u>use</u> to live in a village before we came to Istanbul.
   We used to live in a village before we came to Istanbul.

1 I didn't used to have piano lessons.

   _____

2 My mother use to read me a story before I went to sleep.

   _____

3 I did used to cry a lot when I was a baby.

   _____

4 I used play with toys.

   _____

5 I didn't used to go to school.

   _____

2 **Complete the sentences with *used to* and these verbs.**

> light ~~play~~ read ride send write

0 Before there were CDs and cassettes, people *used to play* their own music.
1 Before cars were invented, people _____ horses.
2 Before we had e-mail, we _____ telegrams.
3 Before houses had electricity, people _____ candles.
4 Before television was invented, people _____ books.
5 Before the telephone was invented, people _____ letters.

3 Write sentences with *used to*.

0 Most people lived in villages 200 years ago.
Most people used to live in villages 200 years ago.

1 People thought the earth was flat.

_____

2 Ancient Egyptians believed in many gods.

_____

3 Dinosaurs existed millions of years ago.

_____

4 People thought the sun went round the earth.

_____

5 Children started work at the age of eight or nine.

_____

6 Men wore hats in the old days.

_____

4 Look at the notes about life 300 years ago and write sentences about what people *used to* and *didn't use to* do.

- go to discos
- live in villages in the country
- look after the animals on the farm
- have computers
- listen to pop music
- walk a very long way to school

0 *People didn't use to go to discos.*

1 _____

2 _____

3 _____

4 _____

5 _____

5 Underline the correct answer.

0 We were **going/used to go** on holiday every summer.
1 Vicky **went to/was going to** dancing lessons when she was young.
2 My father **smoked/used to smoked** before the doctor told him to stop.
3 Tom **was playing tricks/played tricks** on his friends all the time.
4 Whales **used to hunt/are not hunted** any more. It's banned.
5 She **didn't used/didn't use** to like sport.

LESSON 4 *Use Your Grammar*

Summaries

- The idea of a **summary** is to write a brief paragraph that gives the **main points** of a longer passage or text.

- Key words or phrases are the ones which you think are the most important in a passage. Choose key words or phrases and use them to write your summary. You don't have to use exactly the same words as in the main passage when you write a summary.

- Remember – **summaries** can make writing easier.

How?
Well, if you start by thinking of the **main points** and the **key words** you want to include in your writing, then you have got the **summary** of your text and you can develop that summary into your complete text. Using **summaries** in this way – as a starting point for your writing – also helps to make sure you don't forget any important points.

1 **Read this text and note down the key words or phrases which are underlined. Use the key words or phrases to write a summary of the text.**

The Dolphin Inn in Penzance in Cornwall in the south west of England is one of the town's oldest buildings and has two ghosts. The best-known ghost is an old seaman who died there many years ago. The seaman's ghostly footsteps have been heard by visitors and one visitor said that she saw the seaman wearing a big old hat. At the back of the house there is a place where a young man was killed in an accident in 1873 and the Dolphin Inn is haunted by his ghost. A young man is often seen in Bedroom 4 and the bed looks as if someone is sleeping there. This happens even when no-one is using the room and the door is locked. Poeple say that the young man's ghost sleeps in this room.

_____

_____

_____

_____

_____

_____

_____

_____

_____

_____

2 **Read the story again of** *The Most Haunted House In The World* **from** *Shine 3 Student's Book.*

In 1863 a new house was built in the village of Borley, about 100 kilometres north-east of London. Soon after the house was finished, strange things began to happen.

The first owner was a man called Henry Bull and he often saw 'The White Lady'. She was a tall white ghost wearing old fashioned clothes. She used to walk down the garden path at night. She also used to frighten the Bull family by looking in through the window when they were having dinner.

Many other unexplained things happened at this time. Every Monday night a ghostly coach and horses used to race up to the front door. But when the door was opened, the coach disappeared. Plates and glasses used to fly about in the kitchen and the family used to hear strange voices and footsteps. On one occasion, the house became full of strange smells.

In 1930 Mr Foster and his wife Marianne moved in. They didn't use to believe in ghosts but they soon changed their minds! Soon after moving in, they found mysterious messages written on the walls. One message said simply 'Marianne, please help.' The Fosters couldn't settle down in the house.

Harry Price, a famous ghost hunter, spent a year studying the house in 1937. He found a place on the first floor called 'the cold spot' which always used to be six degrees cooler than the rest of the house. On the top floor, doors used to lock and unlock themselves, and furniture used to fall down the stairs. In one bedroom, the Blue Room, people used to be thrown out of their beds at night! Even the bathroom was haunted. A woman going past the door was given a black eye when an invisible hand slapped her face.

In 1939 the house was burnt down in a fire. By then, people had reported seeing over 200 ghosts there. Nothing is left today of what used to be the most haunted house in the world – except ghost stories and a lot of unanswered questions!

3 **Underline what you think are the key phrases and words in the story. Use your key words to write a summary of the story.**

_____

_____

_____

_____

_____

1 Write Tina and Jenny's conversation in reported speech.

0	**Jenny:**	Hi, Tina! How are you feeling?
00	**Tina:**	I'm much better now. I had a terrible cold.
1	**Jenny:**	Lots of things have happened while you were away.
2	**Tina:**	What's happened? Tell me.
3	**Jenny:**	A new girl is coming to school and she'll be in our class.
4	**Tina:**	Where was she before she came here?
5	**Jenny:**	She lived in a village in the country.
6	**Tina:**	Is she nice?
7	**Jenny:**	I don't know. I haven't met her yet.
8	**Tina:**	Has anything else happened?
9	**Jenny:**	Yes, Mr Benson is ill. He's going to be away for two days.
10	**Tina:**	Will we miss our maths lessons?
11	**Jenny:**	No, another teacher is coming today.
12	**Tina:**	We'd better hurry up and go to class.

0   *Jenny asked Tina how she was feeling.*

00   *Tina said she was feeling much better and that she had had a terrible cold.*

1   _____

2   _____

3   _____

4   _____

5   _____

6   _____

7   _____

8   _____

9   _____

10   _____

11   _____

12   _____

2 The Grundy family have been burgled. Report the questions the police asked them.

0   'Do you feel calm enough to answer our questions?'

    The police wanted to know if we were calm enough to answer their questions.

1   'What time did you discover the break-in?'

    _____

2   'Did you lock the house before you left?'

    _____

3   'How long were you out of the house?'

_____

4   'Have you touched anything in the house?'

_____

5   'What did the burglar steal?'

_____

6   'Will you come to the police station tomorrow?'

_____

3 Make sentences with the verbs *see, hear, feel, watch.*

0   audience/clap
     I hear the audience clapping.

1   waves/splash

     _____

2   children/paint a picture

     _____

3   wind/blow

     _____

4   church bells/ring

     _____

5   athletes/run a race

     _____

6   sun/burn my skin

     _____

7   music/play

     _____

4 Write sentences with *used to* or *didn't use to.*

0   He doesn't like fish any more.
     He used to like fish.

1   They don't live in the city now.

     _____

2   They often eat in restaurants now.

     _____

3   She doesn't eat a lot of chocolate these days.

     _____

4   The boy has two pets, not one any more.

     _____

5   I am very happy these days.

     _____

6   She is married now.

     _____

7   She feels calm before exams these days.

     _____

5 Underline the correct answer.

0   I **used to read/used to reading** a lot of books, but now I don't have time.
1   Can you see Maria **to wave/waving** at us from the window?
2   She asked me where I **have/had** been.
3   She told me that she **was getting/got** the bus to school every day.
4   My father **used to cycle/was cycling** to work every day.
5   Have you ever watched dolphins **to swim/swimming** in the sea?
6   She **told me/told to me** to leave.
7   People **didn't use/didn't used** to have televisions and videos.

LESSON 1 *What would you do?*

Second conditional

We use the second conditional to talk about unlikely or unreal present or future situations. We can also use *If I were you I'd...* to give advice.

How do we make the **second conditional**?
We use **if** just like we do in the **first conditional**.
We use the **past simple tense** of the verb in the **if** clause.
We use **would** + the **infinitive** of the main verb (without **to**) in the main clause.
   If I won a competition, I **would** be very happy.
   She **would** scream **if** she saw a ghost.
   If I were you, I'd get another computer.

---

1 Match.

	A			B
0	If my friend were upset,	*d*	a.	she would keep in touch.
1	Would you tell the teacher	☐	b.	would you stop working?
2	If he weren't so short,	☐	c.	if you saw a student copying?
3	Would your dog attack	☐	d.	~~I would try to cheer him up.~~
4	Where would you go	☐	e.	I would ignore that horrible girl.
5	If Sarah moved to a different city,	☐	f.	he would become a basketball player.
6	If you suddenly got rich,	☐	g.	if we won the competition.
7	They would have to walk	☐	h.	if you felt like eating out?
8	If I were you,	☐	i.	if it saw a stranger in the house?
9	It would be fabulous	☐	j.	if their car broke down.

2 Put the words in the correct order to make sentences.

0   in trouble tell would a lie you you were if
   Would you tell a lie if you were in trouble?

1   try I you If harder were would I
   _____

2   grumpy everybody he so him like if would weren't
   _____

3   be would it Sunday I at home if were
   _____

4   alone Mark he miserable wouldn't be if weren't
   _____

5   be if in time I didn't me wouldn't wake for school
   my mother
   _____

6   you would had what you call it if a dog
   _____

3 Complete the sentences with the second conditional.

0   What *would you do* if you saw an alien? (do)

1   If _____ a bag in the street, he would give it to the police. (find)

2   I would help you if _____ the time. (have)

3   If she lost her dog, she _____ another one. (not get)

4   Nick would like watersports if he _____ how to swim. (know)

5   If I _____ more, I wouldn't be so tired. (sleep)

6   _____ if you saw a ghost? (panic)

7   If _____ a mistake, what would you do? (make)

8   If _____ to university, you would get a better job. (go)

9   I _____ healthier if I ate more fruit and vegetables. (be)

10 What _____ if they saw you in those clothes? (say)

4 Complete the second sentence so it means the same as the first one. Use the word in brackets.

0   He doesn't eat very much and he's very thin. (more)

    If he *ate more, he wouldn't be* so thin.

1   She is nice and has lots of friends. (nice)

    If she weren't _____ lots of friends.

2   I'm very busy so I won't go to the cinema. (busy)

    If I _____ go to the cinema.

3   It is raining and we can't go out. (raining)

    If it wasn't _____ go out.

4   He doesn't study and doesn't get good marks. (harder)

    If he _____ good marks.

5   I can't buy the house because it isn't for sale. (would)

    I _____ for sale.

6   He is lonely because he doesn't have many friends. (more)

    He wouldn't _____ friends.

7   The girl is so shocked that she doesn't know what to say. (weren't)

    If the girl _____ what to say.

8   The tourist doesn't speak English and doesn't understand you. (would)

    If the tourist _____ understand you.

5 Complete the sentences. Use your imagination.

1   If I found a bag on the bus, _____

2   If I damaged my friend's bicycle, _____

3   If I didn't pass a test at school, _____

4   If I forgot my mother's birthday, _____

5   If my sister or brother were rude to me, _____

6   If I didn't want to go to school, _____

7   If my friend lost my favourite CD, _____

8   If I saw a burglar in my home, _____

LESSON 2 We can't let him drown!

---

❶ Make/let + object + infinitive

make = force someone to do something
let = allow someone to do something
   Mum **made** me write a letter to Aunt Mabel.
(I didn't want to, but I had to because mum said so.)

   Mum **let** me go to the party later that night.
(Mum said I could go to the party later that night.)

   After both **make** and **let** we use an **object pronoun** (*me, you, him,* etc.) and then the main verb in the **infinitive** without **to**.
   He **made** me do his homework.
   They **let** him go on the school trip.

❷ Allowed to

We can use **allow + object + infinitive** instead of let. This is more formal.

Allowed to is the **passive** form of **let**.
   My parents **let** me go to the party.
   I **was allowed** to go to the party.

When we use **allowed to** we must use the full **infinitive** after it (with **to**).

---

1   Match.

	A				B	
0	We aren't allowed	*d*		a.	allow us to talk in class.
1	You can't make me	☐		b.	people touch the whales and dolphins.
2	Her mum always makes her	☐		c.	see my friends on Saturday.
3	I'm sure Mum will let me	☐		d.	~~to drive fast in the city centre.~~
4	Dad let me have	☐		e.	tell you my secret.
5	At Sea World they let	☐		f.	my own TV and video.
6	Are you allowed	☐		g.	let him go home.
7	The teacher does not	☐		h.	do her homework.
8	When he was better, the doctor	☐		i.	to stay up late at the weekend?

2   Complete the sentences with the correct form of *make, let* or *allow*.

0   You have to get up early tomorrow. I won't *let* you stay up late.

1   'I will _____ you tell the truth,' Tina said to her boyfriend.

2   Don't _____ the dog come into the house! He's dirty.

3   I'm so tired! Please _____ me have a short break!

4   The clowns _____ us laugh with their funny tricks.

5   Visitors are not _____ to take pictures in the museum.

6   Horror films _____ me feel so scared that I can't sleep.

3 Write sentences about teachers at your ideal school. Use *make* or *let*.

0   wear uniforms (not)
They don't make us wear uniforms.

1   bring our bicycles to school
_____

2   wear jewellery to school
_____

3   use mobile phones in class (not)
_____

4   help younger students
_____

5   do jobs for them like shopping (not)
_____

6   play noisy games during breaks
_____

7   do homework (not)
_____

8   discuss our problems
_____

9   chew gum in class (not)
_____

4 Complete the second sentence so it means the same as the first one. Use the word in brackets.

0   We're not allowed to bring electronic games to school. (let)
The teachers *don't let us bring* electronic games to school.

1   I have to eat all my dinner. (makes)
My mum _____ all my dinner.

2   We stayed inside because the weather was bad. (made)
The bad weather _____ inside.

3   The headmaster doesn't allow students to run in the corridors. (let)
The headmaster _____ in the corridors.

4   You mustn't smoke in hospitals. (allowed)
You're not _____ in hospitals.

5   They don't allow you to feed the animals in the zoo. (let)
They don't _____ the animals in the zoo.

5 Underline the correct answer.

0   My dad makes me _____ hard.
a. to study   b. <u>study</u>   c. studying   d. studies

1   My friend lets me _____ games on his new computer.
a. to play   b. playing   c. play   d. plays

2   You aren't _____ to park outside this building.
a. allow   b. allowed   c. let   d. make

3   The children aren't _____ to write on their desks.
a. allowed   b. let   c. made   d. be allowed

4   The teacher _____ them take tests every week!
a. allows   b. to let   c. makes   d. make

5   He tells funny stories to _____ us laugh.
a. let to   b. make   c. allow to   d. make to

6   The skiing instructor makes his pupils _____ hard.
a. trains   b. train   c. to train   d. trained

LESSON 3 | *We'd better tell the others*

---

1 *should(n't)* and *ought(n't) to*

Both **should(n't)** and **ought(n't)** have similar meanings and we can use them in sentences in **present** or in **past** tenses.

We use both phrases when we want to give **advice** to someone.

She **should** work harder.
You **shouldn't** be so rude to your friends.
They **ought to** work harder.
You **oughtn't** to be so rude to your friends.

With **should** we use the **infinitive** without **to**.
With **ought** we use the full **infinitive** with **to**.

2 *Had better*

We usually use **had better** to give advice in specific situations rather than giving general advice. We often use **had better** for situations that are happening now, at the time of speaking.

It's really cold today. You**'d better** take your coat with you.
You're going to be late. You**'d better** not waste any more time.

We use the **infinitive** without **to** with **had better**.
That bread is old. You**'d better** throw it away.

Top Tip!

Both **should** and **ought** are quite like **must**. BUT we use **should** and **ought** for advice and people might or might not take our advice. **Should** is not as strong as **must**.

---

1 Complete the sentences with *should* or *ought*.

0 You *ought* to go to bed earlier.

1 He _____ to take part in the competition. I'm sure he'll win it.

2 You _____ tell them the good news.

3 Mark _____ be nicer to other people.

4 She _____ to ring her parents more often.

5 You _____ to be ashamed of yourself for telling lies.

6 Windsurfing is fun and you _____ to try it some day.

7 _____ I wait for you while you finish the work?

2 Complete the sentences with *had better* and these phrases.

| wear warm clothes   answer it   take an umbrella   hurry   let it cool down   ~~turn on the lights~~ |

0 It's dark. *You'd better turn on the lights.*

1 It's raining. _____

2 The bus is coming! _____

3 It's freezing outside! _____

4 The food is too hot! _____

5 The phone is ringing! _____

3 **Complete these sentences with** *should(n't), ought* **or** *had better.*

0   You *shouldn't* speak like that to your brother.

1   They _____ to work harder to pass the exams.

2   Knives can be dangerous. You _____ to be careful when using them.

3   If you have an exam tomorrow, you _____ to study hard.

4   Their house is on fire! We _____ call the fire brigade at once.

5   You _____ go out without telling your parents where you're going.

6   The boy has fallen off his bicycle! We _____ go and help him.

7   You _____ interrupt me when I'm speaking on the phone.

4 **Complete the dialogue with** *should(n't), ought* **or** *had better.*

Mrs Benson: My son is late! What (0) *should* I do?

Sarah: Don't worry! He (1) _____ be here any moment. He probably stopped to buy something.

Mrs Benson: But it's not like him to be late. If he doesn't come soon, I think I (2) _____ call the police.

Sarah: Maybe he went to a friend's house. I think you (3) _____ to stay calm.

Mrs Benson: I rang his friend Tom, but he didn't go to school today and he hasn't seen John.

Sarah: I'm going upstairs to the bathroom.

Mrs Benson: I think I (4) _____ make a nice cup of tea before I decide what to do.

Sarah: Mrs Benson, I think you (5) _____ to come upstairs and see something.

Mrs Benson: What is it?

Sarah: I think you (6) _____ to see for yourself.

Mrs Benson: Oh look! It's Tom! He's asleep in his bed. Did he come home before me?

5 **Underline the correct answer.**

0   You _____ phone your Mum or she'll be worried about you.

   a. would better   b. <u>had better</u>   c. should better

1   _____ I pay you now or wait until tomorrow?

   a. Should   b. Ought to   c. Shouldn't

2   You really ought _____ her the truth.

   a. to tell   b. tell   c. telling

3   You'd better _____ leave now. It's raining.

   a. not to   b. to   c. not

4   Are we allowed _____ home early today?

   a. go   b. to go   c. to going

5   We _____ to finish our homework before we watch television.

   a. ought   b. must   c. can

6   You _____ try on shoes before you buy them.

   a. shouldn't   b. ought   c. should

6 DOING THE RIGHT THING

LESSON 4 — *Use Your Grammar*

1 Second conditional

We are sometimes asked to imagine what we will do in a specific situation. Now you know how to answer questions like this. By using the **second conditional** you will be able to say how you would react if you were faced with imaginary situations.

Remember that when you use **would** it must be followed by the **infinitive** without **to**.
> If I saw a ghost, I **would** run away very quickly!

2 Advice

Now you know how to give **advice** in lots of different ways.
You have learnt all these words and phrases:
> **should/shouldn't**
> **ought/oughtn't**
> **had better**
> **do/don't**
> **If I were you, I would ...**

1 Answer the questions about yourself.

1 If you had a serious problem, who would you go to for help?

_____

_____

2 What would you say if your friend gave you an awful birthday present?

_____

_____

3 If your friend told you a secret, what would you do?

_____

_____

4 How would you help your friend if he/she were in trouble with his/her parents or at school?

_____

_____

5 Is there anything you wouldn't do for your best friend?

_____

_____

62

2 **Read the letters to the problem page in a magazine and then write answers saying what you think they should do.**

Dear Jane

Dear Jane,

I have a serious problem. Please tell me what you think I should do. My best friend told me that she stole some money from our teacher. She asked me not to tell anyone, but I know that it is wrong to steal. What should I do? What would you do in my place? Please help,

Mary

Dear Jane,

My best friend, Sarah, really likes a boy in our class called James. He is very good-looking and very nice and he is kind to everyone. Sarah told me how much she likes him and she wants to go out with him. There is a serious problem and I don't know what to do about it. James likes me and I like him, too. What should I do? I don't want to hurt my best friend but I want to go out with James. Please tell me what to do,

Julie

Dear Jane,

I am a twelve year old girl and I have a brother who is fourteen. My problem is that every time I try to do my homework my brother plays noisy computer games and I can't study. Our flat is very small and there is nowhere else I can do my homework. My teachers say that I have to work harder, but I don't know what to do. What would you do if you were me?

Sue

Test Yourself

1 Complete the sentences with the second conditional.

0   What would you *say* (say) if someone *gave* (give) you a surprise birthday party?

1   If they _____ (welcome) the new student warmly, she _____ (not feel) lonely.

2   What _____ (you do) if a fire _____ (break) out in your school?

3   If people _____ (use) bicycles instead of cars, there _____ (be) less pollution.

4   If Sarah _____ (do) her homework more carefully, she _____ (get) better marks.

5   If hunters _____ (not kill) so many wild animals, there _____ (be) many more of them.

6   If Nick _____ (ask) Jenny out, _____ (she go)?

7   If I _____ (be) you, I _____ (eat) more fresh fruit and vegetables.

8   If you _____ (shout), they _____ (hear) you.

2 Complete the sentences with the second conditional and your own ideas.

0   If farmers *didn't use* (not use) chemicals, *the fields would be cleaner* _____

1   If people _____ (recycle) paper, _____

2   If we _____ (drive) electric cars, _____

3   We _____ (have) less rubbish if we _____

4   People _____ (not get) ill if they _____

5   If we _____ (protect) wildlife more, _____

6   We _____ (save) energy if we _____

3 Underline the correct answer.

0   If I were their mother, I would **make/let** them tidy their rooms.

1   People shouldn't **to light/light** fires near forests.

2   We're not **let/allowed** to bring mobile phones to school.

3   You **should/ought** to wash your hands before eating.

4   Would the dog attack if you **would tell/told** it to?

5   Travelling by ship makes some people **feel/to feel** sick.

6   If I knew how to swim well, I would **became/become** a lifeguard.

7   You **had should/better** wear old clothes because you will get dirty.

8   You **had better/ought to** phone your parents if you're going to be late.

9   The dog doesn't **let/allow** anybody to go near her food.

4 Complete the sentences with the correct form of *make, let* or *allow*.

0   Will you *let* me have some more chocolate?

1   Her parents don't _____ her have a pet.

2   Julie _____ her friend copy her homework.

3   Young people aren't _____ to buy cigarettes.

4   We _____ some animals unhappy when we keep them in zoos.

5   _____ me do the cooking tonight. You need a rest.

6   She isn't _____ to go out because she's got a cold.

7   He _____ people angry when he shouts.

8   Greenpeace wants to _____ people understand the dangers of pollution.

9   Do your parents _____ you to stay out late?

10 Do mice _____ you feel afraid?

5 Complete the sentences with *should(n't), ought* or *had better*.

0   You *ought* to go the dentist about your tooth.

1   She _____ eat sweets because she's on a diet.

2   You _____ talk while what your teacher is talking.

3   If your dad wants to give up smoking, you _____ to help him.

4   It's very hot in here! I _____ open the window.

5   The baby is asleep. You _____ keep quiet or she'll wake up.

6   'I think you _____ to take some time off work,' the doctor said.

7   He _____ hurry up or we'll miss the beginning of the film.

8   There's a fire. We _____ call the fire brigade immediately.

6 Finish these sentences in your own words.

1   My parents make me _____

2   My English teacher makes me _____

3   I make my brother or sister _____

4   My parents let me _____

5   My parents don't let me _____

6   My parents don't make me _____

7   My best friend lets me _____

8   I am not allowed _____

7 ESCAPE

LESSON 1 *He should have known better!*

1 Should(n't) have

We can use **should(n't)** with **have** + the **past participle** of the main verb to criticise people for things they have or haven't done.

go	**should(n't) have gone**
be	**should(n't) have been**
see	**should(n't) have seen**
open	**should(n't) have opened**

You should have been more careful.
You shouldn't have eaten so much last night.

Note that we can also use **ought(n't) to have** (not **ought to haven't**).

2 Review of reported speech

We use **reported speech** to report what other people said in the past.
Because the **direct speech** was in the past, all the verbs are in past tenses and we change some time expressions to the past as well.

These are some of the **changes**:

present simple	**past simple**
past simple	**past perfect**
present perfect	**past perfect**
will	**would**
can	**could**
last night	**the night before**

"I have been to England."
He said he **had been** to England.

"I went to the cinema last night."
He told me he **had been** to the cinema **the night before**.

We use **told** when we want to include who the direct speech was said to.
He **told** her that he liked her new hair cut.
He **said** that he liked her new haircut.

---

1 Write sentences saying what people *did* or *didn't* do.

0 You should have got up early.
You *didn't get up early*.

1 The boy should have rung his parents.
He _____

2 Nick shouldn't have left without saying goodbye.
He _____

3 They shouldn't have blamed you for the accident.
They _____

4 He should have had breakfast before going to school.
He _____

5 They should have paid attention to you.
They _____

66

2 Write what they *should* or *shouldn't have* done.

0 He lied to his sister.

   He *shouldn't have lied to his sister.*

1 You didn't listen to my advice.

   You _____

2 Grace kept the money she found.

   She _____

3 They brought the dog into the restaurant.

   They _____

4 He didn't finish the work on time.

   He _____

5 The student spoke loudly in the library.

   He _____

3 Complete the sentences with reported speech.

0 'I have never been to France.'

   She said that she *had never been to France.*

1 'We aren't allowed to take pictures in the museum.'

   Sarah said that we _____

2 'I've already had lunch so I'm not hungry.'

   John said that he _____

3 'My dog is very lazy and won't learn any tricks.'

   The little boy said that his dog _____

4 'The students didn't do very well in the test.'

   The teacher said that the students _____

5 'Joe doesn't like getting wet.'

   Stella said that Joe _____

6 'We are going to jump out of the plane soon.'

   The instructor told us that _____

7 'The children enjoyed visiting the zoo yesterday.'

   She said that the children _____

8 'I promise that I will help you.'

   My friend promised that she _____

9 'John has been on holiday since Monday.'

   She told me that John _____

10 'I want you to lay the table.'

   Mother told me that she _____

4 Complete the sentences with *said* or *told*.

0 The teacher *told* the students to be quiet.

1 The reporter _____ many people had been injured in the flood.

2 I _____ you that lunch would be ready soon.

3 He _____ his mother he was getting married.

4 Vicky _____ she wanted to travel all over the world.

5 We _____ him the news.

6 Nick _____ he didn't know the answer.

7 He _____ me it was one o'clock.

8 They _____ they couldn't come with us.

9 She _____ the children a story.

LESSON 2 *I wanted it to go on for ever*

---

❶ Verb + object + infinitive

These verbs can be followed by an **object + to + infinitive**:
   allow   ask   invite   mean   need   promise   teach   tell   want
   I want **you to go** to the supermarket. (**you** = object; **to go** = infinitive)

They **allowed** us to go out.
We **invited** them to spend the weekend with us.
She **wants** you to bring her some milk.
She **told** us to cook dinner.

> **Top Tip!**
>
> **make** and **let** are also followed by an object.
>   He **made** me wear that old shirt.
>   We **didn't let** him play with the dog.

❷ Revision of reported questions

Verbs in **reported questions** are not in their question form. They are in the **affirmative**.
We **don't** use a question mark in **reported questions**.
We can use reporting verbs that show that we are reporting a **question**.
We use **question words** or the word **if** for *yes/no* questions in **reported questions**.
We change the **tense, personal** and **possessive pronouns**, and **time words and phrases** just like we
do in **reported statements**.
   "Did you enjoy the concert last night?"
   I asked her **if** she enjoyed the concert last night.

---

1   Complete the sentences with these words.

| ~~you~~   me   him   her   us   them |

0   I want to invite *you* to my party on Saturday. Can you come?

1   Sally's teacher wants _____ to work harder.

2   Their parents don't allow _____ to watch TV every night.

3   My mum doesn't let _____ stay out late.

4   Our dad makes _____ wash the car every Sunday.

5   The girl he likes told _____ she didn't want to see him.

2 Report these questions.

0 'What time is the film on?' Philip wanted to know *what time the film was on.*

1 'Have you ever been abroad?' He asked me _____

2 'Did you know that Tom can't swim?' They asked _____

3 'When is the train leaving?' The passengers wanted to know _____

4 'What is your name and address?' The police wanted to know _____

5 'Where are you from?' We asked the new student _____

6 'Do you have time to do your homework?' The teacher asked us _____

3 Write the questions the people actually asked.

0 Sally wanted to know what time the lesson started.
'What time does the lesson start?'

1 The child asked if she could have another ice cream.

_____

2 The teacher asked the students if they had all done their homework.

_____

3 The police wanted to know where the money was hidden.

_____

4 My teacher asked me why I had been late that morning.

_____

5 The children wanted to know if they could go out to play.

_____

6 The detective asked us what we had been doing at the time of the murder.

_____

4 Complete the dialogue.

Tom: So how was your holiday, Mike? I (1) _____ your sister and she (2) _____ you had a wonderful time.

Mike: It was fantastic! It was the first time my parents (3) _____ me go on holiday on my own!

Tom: Where did you go?

Mike: We first (4) _____ to Paris and then a friend invited (5) _____ to go to Rome. There I met a beautiful girl, Karen.

Tom: Wow!

Mike: She (6) _____ to know what time it (7) _____ and then we started talking. I invited (8) _____ to visit (9) _____ in London!

Tom: Is she coming?

Mike: Well, she (10) _____ me she (11) _____ think about it!

LESSON 3 *He couldn't do anything!*

❶ Past ability: *could(n't), was(n't)/were(n't) able to, managed to/didn't manage to*

We use these phrases when we want to talk about what a person could or could not do in the **past**.

When I was young I **could** ride a horse.
When I was young I **was able** to ride a horse.

We use **could** to show past ability and also to show somebody had permission for something.

Mum said I **could** have a new computer.

Was/were able to is the **past** form of the phrase **be able to**, and we use it to show someone had the ability to do something in the **past**.
We use **could** to show past ability.

We can **only** use **is/was/were able to** to talk about ability. It is more formal than **could** and it is used much less often.

We use **managed to** when somebody isn't generally able to do something but was able to do it on a specific occasion.

He can't swim but he **managed to** get out of the river safely.

❷ Purpose: *in order to, so that*

We use these phrases to show the **goal** or **purpose** of an action.

He came to England **in order to** see his friends.
He came to England **so that** he could see his friends.

Note that we can use either form when the subject is the same. When the subject is different we use **so that**:

Frank stopped the car **so that** the children could have a drink.

❶ Underline the correct answer.

0 When he was younger the old man **was able/<u>could</u>** hear better.

1 She waved her hand and **managed to/could** attract her friends' attention.

2 The drowning boy **managed/could** to shout for help and was saved.

3 He can't stand meat and so he **couldn't/wasn't able** to eat the dinner.

4 The garage **could/managed to** repair our car quickly, so we continued our trip.

5 We **weren't able/couldn't** read or write before we went to school.

6 We **couldn't/managed** travel fast before cars were invented.

7 Although he lost his job, he **could/managed to** find another one.

2 Complete the sentences with *in order to* or *so that*.

0 He opened his umbrella *in order to* keep dry.

1 The teacher gave us the tests back _____ we could see our mistakes.

2 She went to the supermarket _____ buy some food and drinks.

3 He checked the brakes _____ make sure they were working.

4 He shouted _____ somebody would hear him.

5 The brave man dived into the sea _____ save the little girl.

6 She went to the bank _____ change some money.

7 There are bus stops at many places _____ people can get on or off.

8 The athlete trained hard _____ become a champion.

3 Rewrite the sentences using *in order to*.

0 He studied hard because he wanted to go to university.
   He studied hard in order to go to university.

1 She put make-up on because she wanted to look different.
   _____

2 The dog barked because it wanted to frighten strangers.
   _____

3 You can use the vacuum cleaner when you want to clean the floor.
   _____

4 I wore my sunglasses because I wanted to protect my eyes from the sun.
   _____

5 She opened the fridge because she wanted to eat something.
   _____

4 Rewrite the sentences using *so that* and the word in brackets.

0 They took off their shoes because they didn't want to dirty the floor. (would)
   They took off their shoes so that they would not dirty the floor.

1 They gave out headphones for the passengers to listen to music. (could)
   _____

2 The teacher stopped the cassette for the students to check their answers. (could)
   _____

3 He ran away quickly because he didn't want the dog to bite him. (wouldn't)
   _____

4 He worked all night because he had to finish the project on time. (would)
   _____

5 She put the ice cream in the freezer to stop it from melting. (wouldn't)
   _____

Use Your Grammar

1 Narratives

When you are writing a **narrative** be clear about a few things before you start.
Note down the actions and events you are going to write about.
Be sure you know the order in which those actions or events happened.
Make a plan which includes all the information you are going to use in your story – it helps you to make sure you haven't forgotten anything.

Use **connecting words** to help your reader to understand the **order** in which things happened in:
first, **next**, **then**, **after that**, **later**, **finally**

2 Check your work!

It is always a good idea to **check** your story after you have written it.
If you spend a bit of time **checking** your work, four things will happen –
   1. you will learn from your mistakes.
   2. you will make fewer mistakes in the future
   3. your English will improve
   4. you will be able to write stories more easily in the future
That's why it's such a good idea!

Here are things to look out for when you **check** your work –
Use a good dictionary and a good grammar book.
Make sure your writing is neat and that other people can read it!
Look at all your punctuation to make sure it is correct.
Check that each paragraph is about a new topic.
Make sure you have used some connecting words.
Finally, read your story again to be sure you have done the best work you can!

1 Complete the story below. Use your imagination!

I was walking home last week. It was a cold, windy night and the rain was falling heavily on the roof of the old house. There were no lights on and it didn't look as if there was anybody inside. But suddenly ...

_____

_____

_____

First I _____

_____

_____

Then something even stranger happened. _____

_____

_____

After that_____

_____

_____

Finally _____

_____

_____

2 **Read the text carefully. There are fifteen mistakes underlined. Correct them in the space below.**

George started <u>to walking.</u> The forest was quite big and although he had been there many times before, he was afraid that he would get lost in the dark. He was also a little bit worried that there might be wild animals out there but he told <u>herself</u> not to be a baby and kept walking. He pretended he was a famous explorer and with every step he went <u>deepest</u> into the forest.

He had no idea where to look for the two boys, but he remembered that one of the places <u>john</u> really liked was a cave half way up the mountain, so he decided to go there first. To get to the cave, you had to cross a river, go behind a waterfall and then walk for another hour up the side of the mountain, which was quite difficult to do in the dark!

Finally, George arrived at the cave. He <u>is</u> cold, tired and a bit wet because he had <u>falled</u> into the river. 'Hello, is anyone here?' he whispered. There was no answer. It was completely <u>light</u> inside. He didn't have a torch because they hadn't been invented yet but he did have a box of matches. He lit an old dry piece of wood and looked around. There was no sign of John and his friend but on the other side of the cave there was an old wooden box that hadn't been there before.

He went over to the box and slowly opened it. When he saw what was inside he thought he must be dreaming. He brought his 'torch' closer to get a <u>worse</u> look and could not believe his <u>ears</u>. The box was <u>empty</u> of gold coins! Big bright shiny gold coins! He started jumping around the <u>boat</u> singing 'I'm rich! I'm rich! I'm going to be famous! And rich! So rich!' George was so excited that he had <u>forgetting</u> all about John.

Suddenly two huge men <u>runned</u> into the cave carrying guns and George <u>saw</u> a voice shout 'Run, George! Run for your life!' But it was too <u>early</u>. The men came towards him and George could not escape. He was trapped in the cave!

0 _____ *walking* _____	5 _____	10 _____
1 _____	6 _____	11 _____
2 _____	7 _____	12 _____
3 _____	8 _____	13 _____
4 _____	9 _____	14 _____

3 **Choose a story that you have already written. Rewrite it with some mistakes in and give it to a friend to correct.**

LESSON 5 *Test Yourself*

1 **Complete the sentences with** *should(n't) have* **and a suitable verb.**

0 You *shouldn't have made* fun of him. He's very sensitive.

1 Why did you fail the exam? You _____ harder!

2 It was your sister's birthday yesterday. You _____ her a present.

3 Bill's mother was upset yesterday. He _____ rude to her.

4 He _____ to the party last night. Look how tired he is this morning!

5 You _____ the plant when I was away. Now it's dead.

2 **Rewrite the sentences using** *should(n't) have.*

0 The student made too many mistakes. (be careful)

The student should have been more careful.

1 Lucy left the front door open. (lock)

_____

2 Bill was very tired in the morning. (stay up)

_____

3 Sally didn't tell the police the truth. (lie)

_____

4 The tourists got lost. (have map)

_____

5 Nick felt sick. (eat 10 cakes)

_____

3 **Rewrite the sentences in reported speech.**

0 'I don't believe in ghosts.'

The man said *he didn't believe in ghosts.*

1 'It's too windy and we can't go sailing today.'

The instructor told us _____

2 'The bad weather spoiled the school picnic.'

The boy told his mother _____

3 'The firemen have arrived and they will put out the fire.'

The man said _____

4 'I hope we won't miss the football match.'

His father said _____

5 'I've already seen this film,' said Jane, 'it was really good.'

Jane said _____

4 Underline the correct answer.

0   The boy taught his parrot _____ hello to everybody.
    a. to tel   b. <u>to say</u>   c. saying

1   I can't make him _____ because he doesn't speak English.
    a. understand   b. to understand   c. to not understand

2   You aren't _____ to touch anything in a museum.
    a. allow   b. let   c. allowed

3   They gave Andy some clues _____ he could find the answer.
    a. in order to   b. so that   c. in order

4   The dog hid his bones _____ nobody could find them.
    a. so that   b. in order to   c. that

5   You shouldn't have _____ up your job. It was a mistake.
    a. gave   b. to give   c. given

6   He wanted to know what time _____.
    a. was it   b. it is   c. it was

7   'Birds fly to the south in winter,' his grandfather _____ him.
    a. said   b. told to   c. told

8   'Why _____ shivering?' she asked, 'It's not that cold.'
    a. are you   b. you are   c. do you

9   Mike should _____ here by now. He's never late.
    a. to be   b. has been   c. have been

10 The drivers _____ to continue their journey because of the snow.
    a. couldn't   b. weren't able   c. were able to

5 Report these questions.

0   'What time did you get home last night?' Mum asked me.
    Mum asked me what time I had got home the previous night.

1   'When are we going to the swimming pool?' the boy wanted to know.
    _____

2   'Have you all done your homework?' the teacher asked the students.
    _____

3   'Did you enjoy the party on Saturday?' Bill asked John.
    _____

4   'Can you help me with my homework?' the boy asked his sister.
    _____

5   'When does the train arrive?' the passenger asked the driver.
    _____

LESSON 1 — He'll have to behave himself!

❶ Order of adjectives

The **correct order** for **adjectives** is:
opinion – size – age – shape – colour.

Of course, you don't have to use all five kinds of adjective every time you write!
But when you do want to use more than one adjective, you must put them in the **correct order**.
 I saw a **wonderful big old red** car.

❷ Future modals: *will/won't have to* and *will/won't be able to*

The future of **must** is **will have to**.
The future of **don't have to** is **won't have to**.
The future of **can** is **will be able to**.
 Tomorrow I **will have to** go to the dentist.
 I won't be able to meet you next week.

Let's look at the **tenses** we know for **modals**:

Present	Past	Future
must = have to	had to	will have to
can = am/is/are able to	could = was/were able to	will be able to

One more thing to **remember**. The verb **have to** changes like the main verb **have**.

Present	Past
I have to./I don't have to./Do I have to?	I had to./I didn't have to./Did I have to?
He has to./He doesn't have to./Does he have to?	

❶ Put the adjectives in the correct order.

0 ancient mysterious white round castle.
 mysterious ancient round white castle

1 black huge young hippo

_____

2 old small peaceful village

_____

3 young beautiful tall model

_____

4 red large expensive roses

_____

5 round old brown table

2 Rewrite these sentences in the future.

0   The police must tell the relatives the bad news.

   The police *will have to tell the relatives the bad news.*

1   We can't go swimming this afternoon because it's too cold.

   We won't _____

2   He must water the plants tomorrow, or they will die.

   He will _____

3   Scientists can't predict earthquakes.

   Scientists won't _____

4   You must take an umbrella because it's going to rain.

   You will _____

5   Tim doesn't have to get up early tomorrow.

   Tim won't _____

3 Underline the correct answer.

0   The shipwrecked sailor **won't have to/ <u>won't be able to</u>** survive for long in the cold sea.

1   In the future aeroplanes **will have to/will be able to** travel at great speeds.

2   You can wear jeans. You **will have to/won't have to** wear smart clothes to the party.

3   You **won't have to/won't be able to** keep the fish fresh without a fridge.

4   He **won't be able to/won't have to** hurry because there's plenty of time.

5   She speaks French so she **won't have to/will be able to** translate the letter for you.

4 Complete the sentences with *will/won't have to* or *will/won't be able to*.

0   The student has a lot of homework and she *will have to* stay up late studying.

1   He's lost his keys. He _____ get into his house without breaking a window.

2   Children under five years old _____ pay on the bus.

3   We _____ cook tonight because we are going to order pizza.

4   His car has broken down, so he _____ to continue his journey tonight.

5   The baby is crying so she _____ feed it quickly.

5 Write two things you *will have to do* next week, two things you *won't have to do* and two things you *won't be able to do*.

1   _____

2   _____

3   _____

4   _____

5   _____

6   _____

LESSON 2 *I'll be thinking of everyone*

Future continuous

We use the **future continuous** for events that will be in progress at a particular time in the future.

We form the future continuous with the auxilary verb **be** in the future tense – **will be** and the ending **–ing** for the main verb.

Affirmative	Negative
I will be travelling	I won't be travelling
you will be travelling	I won't be travelling
he will be travelling	he won't be travelling
she will be travelling	she won't be travelling
it will be travelling	it won't be travelling
we will be travelling	we won't be travelling
you will be travelling	you won't be travelling
they will be travelling	they won't be travelling

Questions

Will you **be** travell**ing** tomorrow at 8 o'clock?
Will she **be** work**ing** this afternoon?

Short answers
Yes, I **will**./No, I **won't**.
Yes, she **will**./No, she **won't**.

Let's compare the **future simple** with the **future continuous**.

Future simple
I **will play** the guitar tomorrow might.
(= general future plan)

Future continuous
I **will be playing** the guitar when you arrive.
(= future continuing action)

Remember!
We use the **future continuous** to talk about actions that will be in progress at the time in the future we are talking about.
　　At six o'clock tomorrow I **will be watching** TV.
They **will be learning** English grammar at five o'clock on Friday.

1 Match.

	A			B
0	The baby will be	c	a.	travelling by train. It's a public holiday.
1	Next week the students will be		b.	be served during the flight?
2	Will you be		c.	~~six months old tomorrow.~~
3	The swimmers will be		d.	training very hard for the Olympics.
4	People won't be		e.	alone or with a friend?
5	Will snacks and drinks		f.	taking their final exams.

2 Complete the sentences with the future continuous of these verbs.

~~do~~　eat　live　sleep　study　travel

0 Robots *will be doing* most of our housework in the future.

1 Students _____ at home with computers to help them.

2 We _____ on the moon in special houses.

3 We _____ pills instead of fresh food.

4 People _____ to other planets in the near future.

5 People _____ not _____ for more than four hours a day.

3 Complete the sentences with the future simple or the future continuous.

0 It's his birthday tomorrow and he *will be* 12 years old. (be)

1 He _____ in the garden all day tomorrow. (work)

2 Don't call Philip early in the morning, he _____. (sleep)

3 'I _____ you forever,' he told the girl. (love)

4 I'm in a hurry so I _____ for you to finish. (not wait)

5 The tourists _____ here for more than two weeks. (not be)

6 The doctor _____ you in a few minutes. (see)

7 _____ your parents _____ for you at the airport? (wait)

8 The pilot told the passengers 'We _____ through some thick clouds for ten minutes before landing.' (fly)

4 Read the advertisement.

● Take the trip of a lifetime to see our fantastic dolphins

● Non-stop flights with Atlantic Air with meals served on the plane

● Luxury coaches take you to the harbour

● 3-hour boat excursion with special guides to find the dolphins

● Visit Green Lagoon Spa

● Drink the Magic Water

● Try the local seafood at a traditional restaurant

● Enjoy the spectactular waterfalls in the National Park

● Back to the capital to admire the architecture

● Return to the UK at midnight

Now write sentences saying what the tourists *will be doing* on the trip.

0 The tourists *will be taking the trip* of a lifetime. (take)

1 They _____ with Atlantic Air. (fly)

2 They _____ to find the dolphins. (go)

3 Then _____ Spa. (visit)

4 At the Spa _____ water. (drink)

5 After that _____ restaurant. (try)

6 They _____ National Park. (enjoy)

7 Finally _____ architecture. (travel)

5 Write three things you think we *will be doing* in 100 years from now and three things we *won't be doing*.

1 _____

2 _____

3 _____

4 _____

5 _____

6 _____

LESSON 3 *It will have been worth it*

Future perfect

We use the **future perfect** to talk about actions that **will/won't have** finished by a specific time in the future.

> By this afternoon I **will have cleaned** my bedroom.

Affirmative
I will have eaten
you will have eaten
he will have eaten
she will have eaten
it will have eaten
we will have eaten
you will have eaten
they will have eaten

Negative
I won't have eaten
you won't have eaten
he won't have eaten
she won't have eaten
it won't have eaten
we won't have eaten
you won't have eaten
they won't have eaten

Questions
Will you **have been** on holiday by Christmas?

Short answers
Yes, I **will**./No, I **won't**.

We can use the word **by** to show the 'time limit' for finishing the action.

> **By** eight o'clock I **will have finished** reading this book.
> **By** next week I **will have written** my school project.
> We **will have visited** Paris **by** next May.

---

1 ## Complete the sentences with the future perfect of these verbs.

> be close deliver disappear ~~have~~ leave waste

0   The children *will have had* their supper by the time the film starts.

1   Many kinds of wildlife _____ in five year's time.

2   The postman _____ the letters by the time we get home.

3   The last nuclear power station _____ down by the year 2020.

4   You had better hurry. The train _____ by the time you're ready.

5   All this hard training _____ worth it if he wins the race.

6   People _____ a lot of our natural resources by 2035.

2 Complete the questions and then write answers about a friend.

0 How many times *will you have eaten* pizza by next month? (eat)
Sarah will have eaten pizza twice.

1 How many hours of television _____ in a week's time? (watch)
_____

2 How many hours of sport _____ in a week's time? (play)
_____

3 How many new English words _____ in a week's time? (learn)
_____

4 How many times _____ by bus in a month's time? (travel)
_____

5 How many hours of homework _____ in a week's time? (do)
_____

3 Write sentences saying how much time we will have spent doing the following things by the time we are seventy years old.

0 sleep – 23 years   *We will have slept for twenty three years.*
1 watch television – 5 years and 303 days   _____
2 go shopping – 1 year and 140 days   _____
3 talk on phone – 180 days   _____
4 cry – 50 days   _____
5 laugh – 1 year and 258 days   _____
6 work – 8-9 years   _____

4 Complete the sentences with *will, be* or *have*.

0 The baby *will be* able to walk soon.
1 'We will _____ cleaned up the mess by tea time, the children promised.
2 Will the film _____ finished by 11 o'clock?
3 This time next month we will _____ swimming in the sea.
4 The weather report says it will _____ warm and sunny tomorrow.
5 Let's go! The shops will _____ opened by now.
6 Philip will _____ teaching people how to swim all summer.

5 Complete the sentences with the future simple, future continuous or future perfect.

0 I bet he *will fall* into the river. (fall)
1 I _____ my second book by this time next year. (finish)
2 At exactly this time next week he _____ over the ocean on his way to New York. (fly)
3 The students _____ a museum all tomorrow morning. (visit)
4 Let's visit Tim. He _____ now. (not study)
5 _____ Mrs Smith _____ here all next year, too? (work)
6 My grandmother _____ a hundred years old next week! (be)

LESSON 4

1 The future

Let's review the **future tenses** you have learned.

Future simple
We can use the **future simple** to say what we hope or predict about the future.
I hope I **won't have to** go to school tomorrow.

We can use the **future simple** for promises.
    I'll write to you every day.

Going to
We can use **going to** for plans and intentions or to talk about the future when we can see from present evidence that something is certain to happen.
    I'm going to visit my grandparents this weekend.
    That car's travelling too fast. It's going to crash!

Present continuous
We can use the **present continuous** for arrangements.
    They**'re getting** married next week.

Future continuous
We can use the **future continuous** for actions that will be happening at a specific time in the future.
    This time tomorrow I **will be flying** to India.

Future perfect
We can use the **future perfect** simple for actions that will or won't be finished by a specific time in the future.
    In two month's time I **will have read** four English books.

2 *However*

However means **but**.
We can use **however** to show that a sentence relates to what has been said before. It is often used to give surprising information.

> **Top Tip!**
> Always put a comma (,) after **However**.

The weather was bad. **However**, we decided to go camping.
He studied very hard. **However**, he failed his exams.

1 Complete the sentences using your own ideas.

1   When I am twenty-four, I will _____ .

2   That little boy is running very fast. He is going to _____ .

3   I love learning English. However, _____ .

4   I am playing _____ tomorrow.

5   At eight o'clock tomorrow morning I will be _____ .

6   On Saturday I'm going to _____ .

7   By nine o'clock this evening I will have _____ .

8   I hope it won't _____ .

9   Will she have done _____ ?

10 I will be _____ .

2 **Read these horoscope predictions and then write some of your own. Discuss your ideas with a friend and plan your work together.**

Virgo
This week is going to be fantastic for all Virgos. If you think happy thoughts, then you will be happy. On Monday someone is going to give you some good news about school. On Tuesday you will get a surprise phone call from a friend you haven't seen for ages. Wednesday will be a very ordinary day but by Thursday, a problem you have been worrying about will have been solved. On Friday you will be thinking about someone special all day and at the weekend you will see that person and you won't have to daydream about them anymore!

Scorpio
Be careful this week with your money. You shouldn't spend too much on silly things you don't need. Don't let your family tell you what to do, especially an older brother or sister. Friday is a good day for a journey and wherever you go, you will have a good time. On Sunday you will be feeling strong and powerful so you will be able to do anything. On Monday you should try to be kind to someone who needs your help. However, don't allow their problems to become your problems.

3 **Write sentences about yourself.**

1. **Write three sentences about what life will be like in your town in ten years' time.**
0 *There **will** be a lot more cars and pollution.*
1 _____.
2 _____.
3 _____.

2. **Write three sentences about what you will be doing in July next year.**
0 *I **will be swimming** in the sea.*
1 _____.
2 _____.
3 _____.

3. **Write three sentences about things which will have happened by next December.**
0 *I **will have grown** taller.*
1 _____.
2 _____.
3 _____.

4. **Write three sentences about what you are going to do next weekend.**
0 *I'm **going to cook** a special meal for my friend.*
1 _____.
2 _____.
3 _____.

4 **Write a short passage about next week. Try to use as many future tenses as possible.**

_____
_____
_____

8

Test Yourself

1 **Complete the sentences with the future perfect of these verbs.**

| disappear | discover | ~~hurt~~ | land | not hear | reach | replace |

0 Before retiring, a football player *will have hurt* himself many times.

1 Scientists _____ other planets by the next century.

2 On this fast boat we _____ the island before we know it!

3 Coins and paper money _____ by the year 2025.

4 Jim _____ the news before he gets back from holiday.

5 I _____ this old computer with a new one by next week.

6 The aeroplane _____ by the time we get there.

2 **Underline the correct answer.**

0 The paint **will have/will be** dried in a few hours.

1 The ships **won't be able/won't able** to sail in the bad weather.

2 The thief will **has got/have got** away by the time the police come.

3 Students won't **studying/be studying** for long. It's nearly Christmas.

4 Jack and Mary **will have/won't have** eaten yet. They're waiting for us.

5 You will **able/have** to be more careful in future with your work.

6 Will that athlete **be/been** taking part in the next Olympic Games?

7 Many animals and plants **have/will have** disappeared in the future.

8 Tourists will **be staying/staying** in luxurious hotels on the Moon.

3 **Rewrite the sentences with the adjectives in the correct order.**

0 I think I'll buy that (*little/lovely/old*) chair.

00 I think I'll buy that *lovely little old* chair.

1 Gisele is a (*beautiful/black/slim*) _____ _____ _____ model.

2 We will be moving to a (*modern/small/uncomfortable*)_____ _____ _____ house.

3 His pet is a (*fat/grey/lazy*) _____ _____ _____ cat.

4 My brother likes (*black and white/boring/old*) _____ _____ _____ films.

5 I'll be going on a (*cheap/last minute/short*) _____ _____ _____ holiday.

4 Complete the sentences with *will/won't be able to* or *will/won't have to*.

0 Tom's been playing with the toy for hours. He *will have to* think of something else to do.

1 Mel Gibson's fans _____ see him in a new film soon.

2 His father is in a hurry and _____ have breakfast with the family.

3 If I were you, I'd get a bicycle so that you _____ walk everywhere.

4 Children under ten years of age _____ enter the competition. They have to be older.

5 We're going to buy a dishwasher so we _____ do the washing-up anymore.

6 You _____ vote when you're 18 years old.

5 Complete the sentences with the future continuous or future perfect.

0 This train is so slow! We*'ll be travelling* until midnight! (travel)

1 The city _____ a new sports centre by next year. (build)

2 Let's go inside. Mum _____ dinner by now. (cook)

3 The rescue team _____ for the missing climber now. (look)

4 I haven't decided yet. I _____ a decision by tomorrow. (make)

5 I _____ a red flower when I see you (hold).

6 Underline the correct answer.

0 This old house will _____ fallen down before anybody buys it.
   a. has   b. <u>have</u>   c. be

1 Before entering class, students will _____ put away their mobile phones.
   a. setting   b. be setting   c. get

2 The couple will _____ ready for the wedding next month.
   a. getting   b. be getting   c. get

3 Will the turtles _____ their eggs on the beach by now?
   a. have laid   b. lay   c. able to lay

4 You _____ able to cool down by taking a swim.
   a. will   b. will be   c. be

5 The workmen won't _____ anything to eat all day.
   a. had   b. be have   c. have had

6 Next month many people _____ taking their holidays.
   a. will be   b. will   c. won't

7 The athlete _____ to run faster in order to break the world record.
   a. will be able   b. have   c. will have

LESSON 1   *I'll have them mended*

> ### Have something done
>
> We use **have something done** when we ask or arrange for someone esle to do something for us.
>   I **have my hair cut** every week.
>   He **had his bicycle mended**.
>
> We make sentences with **have something done** with **have + object + past participle**:
>   I **had my house painted**.
>   She is **having her computer repaired**.

1 Underline the correct answer.

0   Lucy loves cooking so she is <u>**preparing the food**</u>/**having the food prepared** for the party.

1   Swimmers often **cut their hair/have their hair cut** very short.

2   She is too poor to **paint her flat/have her flat painted**.

3   He is too lazy to **clean his house/have his house cleaned**.

4   Babies are lucky because they **do everything themselves/have everything done for them**.

5   Mike is **piercing his ear/having his ear pierced** tonight.

2 Complete the sentences with the correct form of *have*.

0   Students *have* their homework corrected by the teacher every day.

1   _____ you ever _____ your nails painted?

2   'When _____ we _____ the broken gate repaired?' he asked.

3   'When are you going _____ the broken window mended?' he wanted to know.

4   'I _____ just _____ the car checked at the garage and they said that it's all right,' she said.

5   She _____ not _____ the garden looked after by a gardener because she loves doing it herself.

3 Complete the sentences with the correct form of these verbs.

do ~~cut~~ dry-clean dye paint print straighten test wash

0   Alison doesn't have her hair *cut* at the hairdresser's very often.
1   Millionaires have their shopping _____ for them.
2   That actress had her nose _____ last year.
3   She isn't having her new house _____. She's doing it herself.
4   Where do you have your photos _____?
5   Are you going to have your winter coat _____?
6   Sarah had her hair _____ very bright red.
7   Did you have your carpet _____ by a professional?
8   I've had my eyes _____ and I should wear glasses.

4 Complete the second sentence so it means the same as the first.

0   Alison's dress was made by her sister.
    Alison *had her dress made* by her sister.
1   An experienced vet examined Philip's dog.
    Bill _____ experienced vet.
2   'Will the flat be painted before we move in?' they asked the owner.
    'Will you _____ before we move in?' they asked the owner.
3   A make up artist usually puts on actors' make-up.
    Actors _____ by a make-up artist.
4   The company had their new office designed by an architect.
    The company's _____ by an architect.
5   A new swimming pool was built so the hotel would attract more tourists.
    The hotel _____ to attract more tourists.

5 Imagine that you are very rich and very lazy. Write five things that you would *have done* by another person.

1   _____
2   _____
3   _____
4   _____
5   _____

LESSON 2 — *What would you have done?*

Third conditional

We use **third conditional** to talk about the consequences of unreal or imaginary past events.
If I **had seen** Tom, I **would have** given him your message.
(But I didn't see Tom, so I didn't give him your message.)

We form the **third conditional** like this: **if + past perfect, would have + past participle**.
If she **had told** me, I **would have had** time to think about it.
They **wouldn't have lost** the match if they **had played** better.

---

1 Match the beginnings with the endings and say if the sentences are second or third conditionals.

A

0   If the skier had been more careful, ☐ *d*

1   Sally would have watched the film ☐

2   If you had chosen a different holiday, ☐

3   If I were you, ☐

4   If the young man had a sports car, ☐

5   He wouldn't have had a fight ☐

6   Nobody would see you ☐

B

a.   if you hid behind that tree. ☐

b.   it would have been better. ☐

c.   if he hadn't been so angry. ☐

d.   ~~he wouldn't have hurt himself.~~ *3rd*

e.   if she hadn't gone to bed early. ☐

f.   I would apologise for being late. ☐

g.   would more girls go out with him? ☐

---

2 Complete the sentences with the third conditional.

0   If I *had known* you were in hospital, I would have visited you. (know)

1   If the cat hadn't eaten so much, it _____ sick. (not be)

2   If you had won the lottery, _____ any money to the poor? (you give)

3   If the little girl _____ afraid, she wouldn't have screamed. (not be)

4   If scientists _____ new medicines, many people would have died younger. (not discover)

5   They _____ the treasure if the old map hadn't shown where it was. (not find)

6   If he _____ you to the party, would you have gone? (ask)

7   If you had studied harder, do you think you _____ the exam? (pass)

3 Complete the sentences with the third conditional.

0   If Lucy *had invited* (invite) me to the party, I *would have gone*. (go)

1   If a reporter _____ (see) the film star, the star's picture _____ (be) in every newspaper.

2   If my girlfriend _____ (miss) me, she _____ (ring) me every day.

3   Your friend _____ (forgive) you if you _____ (apologize).

4   If the student _____ (spend) more time studying, he _____ (get) better marks.

5   Alison _____ (cook) something if she _____ (know) you were coming.

6   If the firemen _____ (not come) quickly, the fire _____ (destroy) the village.

7   If I _____ more time (have), I _____ (watch) the film last night.

8   The boy _____ (be) so tired if he _____ (go) to bed earlier.

4 Complete the second sentence so it means the same as the first.

0   She didn't believe in herself and so she felt nervous.

If she *had believed in herself, she wouldn't have felt nervous.*

1   The young actor starred in the film and became famous overnight.

If the _____

2   The children didn't enjoy swimming because the water was so cold.

The children would _____

3   Jack and Susan didn't have their own house and had to live with Jackie's mother.

If Jack and Susan had_____

4   Paul shouted at his boss, and so he lost his job.

If Paul _____

5   Mark didn't have enough money, so he didn't go to the fair.

If Mark had _____

6   They ate two huge pizzas for dinner and then felt sick.

If they _____

9 TEAM CHALLENGE

LESSON 3   *He can't have done!*

---

1 *Must/can't have* **for deduction**

Remember that we can use **must** to show that we are sure that something is true and **can't** to show that we are sure something is not true.

   This **must** be Martha. She said she was coming at eleven.
   Jim's on holiday this week so he **can't** be at his office.

We can use **must/can't have** to make deductions about the **past**. **Have** is followed by the past participle.

   It's only eleven o'clock. Those children **must have finished** school early today.

Note that we use **can't** as the opposite of **must**.

   It **must have been** Mary who called him last night.
   No, it **can't have been** Mary, because she has gone on a camping trip.

2 *Could/may/might have* **for speculation**

We use **could/may/might have + past particple** when we are guessing about what possibly happened in the past. **Have** is followed by the past participle.
We use **could** when we think something is probable.
We use **may** when we are not so sure.
We use **might** when we are less sure but we think something is possible.

   Where has Tom gone?
   Simon is fairly sure he knows where Tom is:
   "He **could have gone** swimming. He loves swimming," said Simon.

   Mary remembers that Tom likes fishing too – but not as much as he likes swimming –
   "Or, he **may have gone** fishing," Mary said.

   Terry thinks of another possibility – but it isn't as probable as the other two ideas.
   "He **might have gone** for a walk," said Terry.

---

1 **Complete the sentences with these verbs in the correct form.**

| be   cost   disappear   go   ~~pay~~   watch   win |

0   The rich woman must have *paid* a lot for that diamond necklace.

1   Where did they get all this money from? They must have _____ the lottery.

2   Mum isn't here. She might have _____ to the shops.

3   I heard a loud bang. It must have _____ a car crash.

4   Millions of people must have _____ the first moon landing in 1969.

5   He can't have _____ into thin air. He must be here somewhere.

6   His education must have _____ his parents a lot of money.

2 Complete the sentences with *must* or *can't*.

0 My sister *must* have taken my new jeans. I can't find them anywhere.

1 Mark was supposed to here by now. Something _____ have happened to him.

2 They _____ have had a fight. They're such good friends.

3 That film is really funny. You _____ have laughed a lot.

4 The boys ate four pizzas. They _____ have been very hungry.

5 He's usually so nice. He _____ have meant to upset you.

3 Complete the sentences with *must have, can't have* or *might have.*

0 He is bleeding. He *must have* cut himself.

1 Turn on the answering machine. Somebody _____ phoned while we were out.

2 The burglars _____ got into the house through the bathroom window. It's open.

3 The guests _____ enjoyed the food. They hardly ate anything.

4 The baby smells lovely. It _____ had a bath.

5 How did the prisoner escape? He _____ climbed over the wall, but I'm not sure.

6 You _____ met him. He died before you were born.

7 Your parents _____ been happy with your good marks.

4 Complete the sentences in your own words.

1 Will has lived here for many years and knows the area well.
He can't have _____

2 Sara and Mario are very good students.
They must have _____

3 Your dog is missing.
It might have _____

4 Our teacher was very pleased with us.
We must have _____

5 Her brother is always honest.
He can't have _____

5 For each sentence write two possible explanations.

0 The boy passed his exams.
  a *He must have studied hard.*   b *He might have been lucky.*

1 She is late for school.
  a _____   b _____

2 They are eating a big cake.
  a _____   b _____

3 I can't find my ring.
  a _____   b _____

4 I don't feel very well.
  a _____   b _____

Use Your Grammar

Modals for deduction and speculation

When we talk about possibility we can use **modals**. Here are the **modals** we have learned:

can
could
may   + **infinitive** without **to** to talk about the **present**
might
must
can't

I **may** buy a new pair of shoes.

can't have
must have
may have   + **past participle** to talk about the **past**
might have
could have

They all look very happy. They **can't have** heard the sad news about George yet.

1 **Underline the correct word(s).**

1   James **must have/might have** gone to the park. I'm not sure.

2   You **could/must** listen to the teacher if you want to understand the lesson.

3   You **might have/can't have** seen my mum in town. She is in hospital today.

4   I think I **can't/might** go to the cinema tonight with Judy.

5   That **could/can** be the man who stole my purse. It looks like him.

6   Do you think it **must/might** snow later?

7   Sarah said she thinks she saw a ghost. She **might/must** have been very frightened!

8   I **can't/must** have passed my exams. I didn't do any revision.

2 **Answer the questions about yourself. Use your imagination if necessary!**

1   What would you have done if you had been given a lot of money for your last birthday?

_____.

2   What would you do if you were asked to sing at a concert?

_____.

3   What will you do if you win the lottery?

_____.

4   What did you do last week?

_____.

5   What must you do to keep fit?

_____.

6   What might you do tomorrow?

_____.

7   What will you do when you finish this exercise?

_____ .

8   What would you do if you had got all these answers right?

_____ .

3   Read episode three of John and George's adventure.

For a few moments George did not know what to do. Here he was, in the middle of the night, trapped in a dark cave with the friends he had been trying to rescue! Some help he had been! 'This can't be happening to me,' he thought, 'I must be dreaming.' He shivered with cold and realised that this was no dream. One of the men had pushed John over next to George and the three boys just looked at the men without speaking.

Both men were tall and well built and looked very strong. They were wearing filthy clothes and hadn't shaved for several days. One of them was really tall with blonde hair and angry looking small brown eyes. The other one had black hair but his eyes were pale greeny blue and cold. 'Just like an animal,' thought George, and shivered again, but this time with fear. Who were, these men and what were they doing in the cave with the box of gold coins?

'Well,' said the black-haired man to George, 'We've been waiting for you. Your friend here said you would have arrived by midnight and he was right. Who are you and what are you doing out on the mountain at this time of night?'

'Don't say anything, John,' John whispered, 'They must be thieves – look at all that gold!'

While the boys were looking at the box of gold, the black-haired man spoke again.

'We know who you are. We know that you are the sons of Scarface Nick. You must have been left here to look after the gold while Scarface and his men went off to steal some more. We've been chasing Scarface Nick for weeks! Now we've got his boys, it'll be easy to catch him, too.'

'Scarface Nick! I've heard of him,' said John. 'Isn't he the famous bank robber that the police have been looking for?'

'What do you mean you've heard of him? You're his sons, aren't you?' said the black-haired man angrily.

John, George and their friend looked at each other and started to explain what had happened and how they had found the gold in the cave. Slowly the men put their guns down and smiled. They told the boys that they were secret agents who had been trying to catch Scarface.

'We must stop him before any more banks are robbed!'

The two agents whispered together for a couple of minutes and then the black-haired man turned round and spoke.

'You must know the mountain and forest really well. If we explained exactly what we need, would you help us or do you want to go back home?'

'Do we want to go home?' George repeated, 'I wouldn't have missed this for anything!'

4   What do you think the secret agents are planning to do? Compare your ideas with a friend and write the final episode of the story.

LESSON 5   *Test Yourself*

1 Write what these people have done for them.

0	a baby/face/wash	*A baby has its face washed.*
1	a model/hair and make-up/do	_____
2	a driver/car/clean	_____
3	an old lady/shopping/carry	_____
4	a small child/face/wash	_____
5	a businesswoman/letters/type	_____

2 Complete the sentences with the second or third conditional.

0   If you *had come* sailing with us, you would have seen the dolphins. (come)

1   If I had time, I _____ you but I'm so busy at the moment. (help)

2   If Tom had run faster, he _____ the bus. (not miss)

3   What would you do if that nice boy _____ you out? (ask)

4   I would wait a little longer for them if I _____ you. (be)

5   If you _____ more sense, you wouldn't have climbed that dangerous mountain. (have)

6   If the students had remembered, would they _____ their teacher a present? (buy)

3 Underline the correct answer.

0   You **can't/must** have lost your keys on the way home or in the shop.

1   Ann **can't have/must** done well in the test. She didn't know a thing.

2   The climber **could/could have** lost his balance when he looked down the cliff.

3   May **can't/might** have taken the dog for a walk, but I'm not sure.

4   It can't **be/have been** Mike you saw in the city centre. He's upstairs sleeping.

5   The millionaire **can't have/must have** chosen the most expensive clothes in the shop.

6   Tara could **has decided/have decided** to leave early.

7   The burglar **can't have/must have** escaped through the front door. It's locked.

4 Complete the sentences with *must/can't/could have* and one of these verbs.

answer	bury	hide	refuse	~~rain~~	snow

0   The roads are wet. It *must have rained* last night.

1   Paul's your best friend. He _____ to help you.

2   Some people think thieves _____ a treasure somewhere on the island.

3   Jenny _____ the phone. She's at school.

4   The police don't know where the thief _____ .

5   Let's go skiing in the mountains. It _____ there last night.

5

5 Complete the sentences with the third conditional.

0 If he *tried* parachuting, I'm sure he *would like* it. (try/like)

1 If I _____ afraid, I _____ for help. (be/not scream)

2 Where _____ if _____ the holiday? (you travel/win)

3 If you _____ yourself badly, _____ to the doctor? (injure/you go)

4 They _____ longer if they _____ the time. (stay/have)

5 If Nick _____ into the freezing water, he _____ a cold. (fall/catch)

6 If I _____ she was so sensitive, I _____ at her. (know/not shout)

6 Complete these sentences in your own words.

1 If I had lost the keys to the front door, _____

2 If someone had damaged my bike, _____

3 I would have been very upset _____

4 If I hadn't studied so hard, _____

5 If I had been able to, _____

6 If the teacher had given us a lot of homework, _____

7 Underline the correct answer.

0 Most people _____ their old clothes repaired. They just buy new ones.
   a. not have   b. haven't   c. don't have

1 The queen _____ everything done by servants.
   a. has   b. have   c. uses

2 If your parents _____ away at the weekend, would you have had a party?
   a. gone   b. had gone   c. go

3 She isn't here. She _____ decided not to come.
   a. can't have   b. could   c. must have

4 When you stay at a hotel, you _____ your bed made for you.
   a. haven't   b. not have   c. have

5 Dad _____ come home. His car is parked outside the house.
   a. can't   b. may has   c. must have

6 The star _____ her dress made by professionals. She made it herself.
   a. hadn't   b. didn't have   c. not have

7 You _____ so many mistakes if you had read the instructions.
   a. made   b. wouldn't have made   c. wouldn't make

8 She's as white as a sheet. She must _____ a ghost!
   a. see   b. have seen   c. saw

95

Macmillan Education
Between Towns Road, Oxford OX4 3PP
A division of Macmillan Publishers Limited
Companies and representatives throughout the world

ISBN 0333 99995 9

First published 2002

Designed by Sofia Flokou.

Illustrated by: Kath Abbot (Specsart); Alan Batson (Specsart);
Mike Bell (Specsart); Roger Blackwell (Specsart); Mark Duffin;
Bob Harvey (Pennant); Gillian Hunt: Tim Kahan: Helen Kidd (posters);
Angela Lumley (Specsart); Mark MacLaughlin; Des Nicholas; Julia Pearson;
Glynn Rees (Specsart); Paul Shorrock; Dan Simpson (Specsart); Gary Slater;
Simon Turner; Christos Varlamas; Roger Wade Walker.

Cover design by Xen Media Ltd

The authors would like to thank Julie Stone and everyone else who helped with this project.

The publishers would like to thank Howard and Hara Middle.

Commissioned photography by: Peter Lake pp6, 7.

Printed and bound in Spain by Edelvives S. A.
2006 2005
10 9 8 7 6 5 4 3